Cover illustration: central panel of the Charles Kingsley
Memorial window from Eversley Church, Hants.
Used with the kind permission of the Churchwardens.
Photograph by Dr Tom Poole. ©The Saint Austin Press.

POVERTY MY RICHES

POVERTY MY RICHES

A Study of St. Elizabeth of Hungary

1207-1231

Elizabeth Ruth Obbard ODC

The Saint Austin Press

This book is dedicated to my FMDM sisters
with love and gratitude
and in honour of the Congregation's Year of Jubilee
1996 - 1997

Nihil Obstat: Canon Paul A. Taylor D.D.
Imprimatur: Mgr. Philip Shryane V.G.

Norwich, 3 August 1997

© 1997, Sr. Elizabeth Ruth Obbard/Carmel of Our Lady of Walsingham. Design of this edition ©1997, The Saint Austin Press, Southampton.

This book is sold subject to the condition that it shall not, by way of trade or otherwise, be lent, re-sold, hired out or otherwise circulated without the publisher's prior consent in any form of binding or cover other than that in which it is published and without a similar condition including this condition being imposed on the subsequent purchaser.

All rights reserved. No part of this publication may be reproduced or transmitted in any form or by any means, electronic or mechanical including photocopying, recording or any information storage or retrieval system, without prior permission in writing from the publishers.

A catalogue record for this book is available from the British Library.

ISBN 1 901157 80 6

Printed in Great Britain by BPC Wheatons, Exeter.

The Saint Austin Press
PO Box 610
Southampton
SO14 0YY

Table of Contents

Author's note   9

Prologue – a Death in the Night   11

1. Two Ways, One Woman   13
2. Infancy   19
3. The World of the Thirteenth Century   23
4. Growing Years   31
5. The Flowering of Love   37
6. Growth in Maturity   43
7. The Unimaginable Anguish   55
8. Franciscan Sister   65
9. Holiness Acknowledged   75
10. Only Love Remains   81
11. Love Purified   87
12. A Heart for the World   95

Appendix: The Present Rule of the Third Order Regular of St. Francis   99

Bibliography   108

Author's note

The sources for the life of St. Elizabeth come mainly from the witnesses at her canonisation process, and especially the testimony of her faithful companions, Guda and Ysentrude. There is also an extant letter that Conrad of Marburg, her Confessor, wrote to the Pope, hoping to interest him in Conrad's saintly penitent. Other chroniclers, like the monks of Rheinhardsbrunn, fill out the picture we have of Elizabeth's husband, Louis and offer other details, some of which seem more plausible than others. I have tried to be as faithful as possible to the original sources as I believe the facts of Elizabeth's life speak far more eloquently than fiction and legend.

Elizabeth is a woman who has a message for our worl, as she had for her own. She tells us of the meaning of love and fidelity, of service and sacrifice. She deserves to be better known. Hence this present book which I hope she will bless.

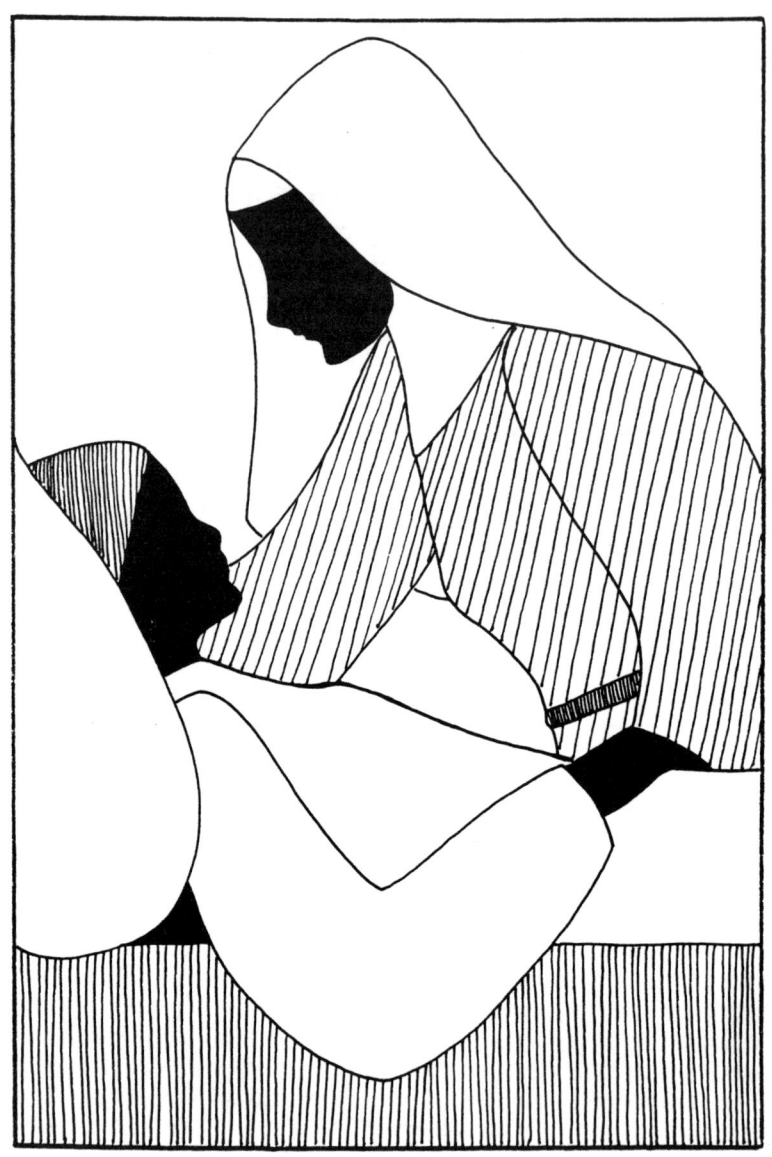

Prologue

A Death in the Night

You have died and your life is hidden with Christ in God. When Christ your life is revealed, then you also will be revealed with him in glory.
Col. 3:3-4

It is November 16th, 1231, and in Marburg, Hesse, a young woman lies dying. Her pallet is laid on a slightly raised platform and she wears a plain shift of coarse, unbleached linen. That morning her director has heard her last Confession and brought Viaticum. Now it is the hour of Vespers. The weak body breathes shallowly, the woman's youthful fragility accentuated by the pale, almost translucent skin contrasting with the rich, blue-black hair cropped close to her head. How different she is from the people with ruddy complexions and fair colouring who watch her.

In the bare room are some Friars Minor whose presence in Germany they owe to this young woman's invitation some years previously. There are also a few Cistercians in their black and white, and two grey-habited Franciscan Sisters from the hospital this woman has founded, and in which she has acted as a nurse for several years. At the head of her bed sits a little boy, his face grubby from crying, his bald skull showing the effects of acute ringworm. This child is the woman's adopted son, cared for with all tenderness ever since she found him cowering in the town gutters.

Of all those present only the boy weeps noisily. The religious keep vigil with a kind of sorrowful fascination, coupled with the scarcely concealed curiosity of the professionally pious.

The woman before them is Elizabeth, daughter of the King of Hungary, widow of the former Landgrave of Thuringia and mother of the heir. At twenty-four, death is coming prematurely. Those watching her hear her singing as if accompanying an invisible bird in a song inaudible to human ears. Her face, as it has been throughout her life, is serene and smiling.

Night draws on and Elizabeth's thoughts turn to another Mother and her Son, born in a poverty such as Elizabeth knows in death. 'Let us speak,' she murmurs,' of God and the Child Jesus, for it will soon be midnight, the hour in which Jesus was born and laid in a manger. And by his Almighty Power he created a star never seen before.' Then she prays for all around her, saying to the sister attending her: 'My dear, the moment has come when God will call his friend to himself.' Then she closes her eyes and lapses into silence.

Midnight passes. In the early hours of November 17th Elizabeth, of royal birth, wife and widow of Thuringia's Landgrave, mother of three children, foundress of the Marburg hospital, dies a Franciscan Tertiary: a poor woman among the very poor, with nothing to call her own.

The religious present begin the Office of the Dead. The scabby boy sobs even louder. Word spreads through the town like wildfire.

From all the area of Marburg, and from miles beyond, the poor converge on the hospital of St. Francis. Weeping and crying out their grief, they acclaim as a saint the woman who has loved them as her own, and identified her life with theirs. She has been for them the reflection of the compassionate Christ's presence among them.

'Elizabeth, our saint Elizabeth!' The dawn echoes with their cries. But the young woman is now for ever silent.

Two ways, one woman

O the depths of the riches and wisdom and knowledge of God! How unsearchable are his judgements and how inscrutable his ways! For who has known the mind of the Lord? Or who has been his counsellor? Or who has given a gift to him to receive a gift in return? For from him and through him and to him are all things. To him be glory for ever. Amen.
Rom. 11:33-36.

In his book, *Christian Vocation*, René Voillaume says that there are two ways of persevering beyond the beginnings in the Christian life. God will either give the gift of contemplation or the gift of deep tenderness for others. This is not a matter of personal choice but of God's choice for us, working as grace does with the nature we have been endowed with. Each one is to reflect Christ in a personal manner, but in each one, prayer or practical compassion will predominate, according to the needs of the Church and the attractions of grace.

In the Old Testament, God appears mainly under two aspects. The first I will designate as God the Lover. Israel, the bride, is the one to whom God looks for a response of love, praise, worship, giving love in return for love. Without this reciprocal love a relationship withers and dies. The second aspect is God as a merciful and compassionate Father or Mother, calling Israel to embody these qualities in a holy way of life that includes justice towards the weak, tenderness towards the widow and orphan, a readiness to forgive and to forge a new society on the personal dignity of each individual.

In the New Testament these two aspects of the divine are blended in the person of Jesus. He reaches out to heal, to console, to forgive, to reassure people of their individual dignity and preciousness, however depraved or sick or sinful they feel themselves to be. This is complemented by nights spent in prayer. He is with the crowds yet he withdraws to solitary places where he passes extended time in silence, in listening love.

John the Evangelist catches some of these intimate movements of the heart of Jesus when he gives us the last

discourse and the high priestly prayer before the Passion.

In a well known saying, John of the Cross writes that in the evening of life we shall be judged on love. Love is to be the core of Christian living but it must be Christlike love. So much passes for love that is merely self-gratifying passion, a using of others to fulfil our own needs regardless of the other's uniqueness and dignity. The path to authentic love is the path where the Christian is open to God in such a way that natural gifts are not suppressed or denied but submitted to deep purification. Only when the ego is displaced can Christ take full possession. The fire of love must burn away all evil until one can say with St. Paul, 'It is no longer I that live, but Christ who lives in me.' The cycle of self-gratification is broken by real love for others and selfless worship of God. In the first way there is a refusal to judge others, a refusal to condemn or manipulate. It is so easy to protect ourselves against criticism by constructing a hard shell around us to deflect the blows and hide our vulnerability. It is easier to put the blame elsewhere instead of facing the truth of the human situation with all its paradoxes and imperfections. Christlike love only begins to surface when, in the day to day struggle of living, we try to put others before self even at personal cost, for a love which costs little is worth little.

This love can take many forms: a passion for justice and the plight of the poor, while refusing to be motivated by hatred of the rich; a call to be identified with the handicapped, the destitute, the sick, or more prosaically a deep inner desire to give oneself to the service of one's small community of family or church.

In all this one allows the heart to be bruised. One has to be ready for actions to be misunderstood while continuing to stretch out hands of kindness, opening one's arms and heart in crucified self-donation.

The second way is one that finds its ambience in silent worship, in searching the depths of God rather than width of outreach to others. It is to go to the solitary place of the heart in prayer and persevere in darkness and aridity. It is to pour out the precious substance of one's life before God in hidden immolation, like the drops of precious ointment poured over the Lord by Mary of Bethany, for 'the poor are always with you, but you will not always have me', says Jesus.

Each dedicated Christian life will have elements of both approaches. The one who reaches out to the needy has to be supported by a prayer life of personal depth in order to sustain self-giving, universal love. Those called mainly to the contemplative approach must still work at personal relationships and struggle to love realistically those with whom they share life. A relationship with God can never be used as an excuse to keep others at bay and deny the messiness of the world as it is.

But while there will be both elements in every life we can be certain that one element will predominate simply because we are limited beings. Speaking of religious orders the Second Vatican Council says:

> Religious should carefully consider that through them, to believers and non-believers alike, the Church truly wishes to give an increasingly clearer revelation of Christ. Through them Christ should be shown contemplating on the mountain, announcing God's kingdom to the multitudes, healing the sick and maimed, turning sinners to wholesome fruit, blessing children, doing good to all and always obeying the Father's will. *Constitution on the Church*, 46

This could equally well refer to individuals. One will reflect the praying Christ, another his compassion for sinners, another his tenderness, his teaching, his healing, all in different degrees according to the grace granted, the present needs of the Church, and natural inclination.

In the history of Israel we can see how men and women were raised up and gifted for the work most needed at a particular time. Moses, Judith and Deborah reflect outgoing, leadership qualities; Rebecca and Ruth the meaning of faithful, domestic love. Amos and Isaiah rally their compatriots to the message of social justice. Each person contributes to the whole and can be a model for those who follow after.

It seems to me that in our day, when there is a tendency in the Church to exalt the enclosed contemplative life as the ideal and to see activity as only a 'second best', it is time to redress the balance by recalling a woman who managed to combine the life of prayer with one of intense activity outside the structures of monastic or conventual life. She was engaged at an early age, married her betrothed at fourteen, yet managed to live a life of contemplation, wide ranging service, and familial devotion which culminated in an early widowhood and four years of chosen poverty and deprivation. She was a woman raised up for her own time, but a woman for all time. Her name was Elizabeth; Elizabeth of Hungary as we call her today, but during her own life known as the Princess Elizabeth, Landgravine and later dowager-Landgravine of Thuringia.

It is given to few to incorporate in one life the heights of contemplation with great activity. Saint Teresa of Avila is an obvious example, but her very outstanding endowments of personality and the universality of her accomplishments can convince her admirers that she is not to emulated by the ordinary person. Her long life, her writings, her business acumen, her grasp of people and affairs, set her apart as a giant among pygmies. Elizabeth is different. Despite her high birth she is more 'localised', more imitable, and therefore more 'one of us.'

Not all can be contemplatives, but all can lead lives of active love. This is required by the Gospel and is incumbent on all. Elizabeth as a woman charts a path that is both a challenge and a pattern for everyone who heeds the words of Isaiah:

> Is not this the fast that I choose . . . to share your bread with the hungry and bring the homeless poor into your house; when you see the naked to cover them, and not to hide yourself from your own kin?
> If you offer your food to the hungry and satisfy the needs of the afflicted then your light shall rise in the darkness, and your gloom be like the noonday. The Lord will guide you continually and satisfy your needs in parched places and make your bones strong; and you shall be like a watered garden, like a spring of water, whose waters never fail.   Is. 58: 7-11

This is a picture of Jesus and a picture of Elizabeth, one who followed him as closely as she knew how: Elizabeth of Hungary.

Infancy

Can a woman forget her nursing child or show no compassion for the child of her womb? Even these may forget, yet I will never forget you. See I have inscribed you on the palms of my hands; your walls are continually before me.
Is. 49:15,16.

Elizabeth died in poverty but she was born to wealth and rank such as few inherit. Her father, Andrew II, of the house of Arpád, succeeded to the throne on the death of his brother Emerich. It had been intended by Emerich that his own son should succeed to the kingdom, with Andrew as regent during his minority. But Andrew had not fought his brother over the years merely for the honour of a regency. Nor was his wife, the grasping Gertrude of Meran, ready to stand meekly aside when the crown was within her reach.

In alarm, Emerich's widow fled to Austria with her child. War was declared, then suddenly the four year old prince simply disappeared. Fighting was discontinued, the heir's mother remarried, and Andrew ascended the throne as undisputed monarch of Hungary. It was 1205.

Two years later Queen Gertrude bore Andrew a baby daughter who was christened Elizabeth. Another royal princess meant another pawn in the marriage markets of the great. Elizabeth already had an older sister, Mary, who in due course was betrothed and married to the King of Bulgaria, and there was a one year old brother, Béla, to secure the inheritance. A noble family would find the new baby a desirable prize as bride for an elder son. Her lineage was impeccable, and her father was anxious to consolidate his claim to the throne by attracting powerful allies. Elizabeth's mother, coming as she did, from a German family, would especially welcome an alliance that would honour her homeland.

The unsuspecting baby girl, smiling and cooing in her cradle, was not only the centre of attention in the Hungarian royal court, but was a precious commodity to bargain with. She, a child with an immortal soul and the power of free choice, was marked out to be traded with as if she were her father's possession, before becoming the possession of her husband and later again, of her sons. All this Elizabeth was to transcend in such a way that she remained true to herself, her individuality, and her unique understanding of her own dignity and destiny. But that was still in the future.

Elizabeth's hand was soon requested by Hermann, Landgrave of Thuringia, for his eldest son and heir, Louis, and it was arranged that Elizabeth would henceforward be brought up at the Thuringian court.

One wonders what, if any, memories the child retained of her native country which she left when she was four years old. Elizabeth would see her father only once more, just after her marriage. Her mother, Gertrude (after whom Elizabeth named her own youngest child, the one destined from birth for the cloister), was murdered when Elizabeth was six.

Gertrude's imprudent intrigues on behalf of her family, to whom she gave positions of power and importance in Hungary, led her to being a hated consort and a bitter adversary to her enemies. Her assassination went unmourned by the majority of the Hungarian people. Elizabeth's heredity was, as with all of us, a mixture of brutality and sanctity, courage and weakness, astuteness and naivety, love and hate.

Elizabeth was a child of her time, a normal child, blessed with a happy disposition and everything that money and rank could offer. The proposed match with Louis of Thuringia seemed ideal. Gertrude was determined that her daughter should be provided with a dowry worthy of a princess, a dowry that would cause her adoptive people to revere the king who could provide his daughter with such riches.

Hermann formally asked for Elizabeth through a special embassy empowered to negotiate terms and bring the future bride back to her new country. The escort was well armed and bore gifts for the Hungarian royal family, as well as everything needful to make the journey homeward as comfortable as possible for the princess. Gertrude, meanwhile, anxious to display the treasures of the Hungarian court and make a favourable impression on the envoys, loaded her daughter with costly garments, silk, brocades, jewellery, spices and a much commented upon silver bath. Two Hungarian priests were in her personal entourage, as well as ladies in waiting, knights and servants. The priests were charged with the task of remaining with Elizabeth in Thuringia to teach her the Christian faith and keep her conversant with her native language and the history of her own land and forebears.

The travelling would have been tiring but exciting for a young child, taking several weeks on the road. There was the necessity for overnight stops en route, there were the frequent changes of scenery, the welcome of various great households and the food and entertainment awaiting her there. And she would meet other travellers, acrobatic performers, troubadours wandering from court to court with their ballads and songs, jugglers, bear trainers, beggars.

Peasants came out from their hovel doors to stare at this king's daughter as she innocently looked about her with inquisitive eyes. Their gaze widened as they noted the loaded wagons, the escort of knights, ladies and men at arms. When Elizabeth was canonised twenty-four years later there were some who still remembered this triumphant cavalcade, with its treasure-laden carriages and its gleaming silver bath displayed for all to see, a royal trophy advertising the presence of a princess who must be tended and cleansed with every ceremony.

At the Thuringian border her new family was waiting for her. Elizabeth was met by Hermann's wife, Sophia, together with Louis and his youngest sister Agnes, a child of Elizabeth's own age. Formalities completed, the betrothal was duly celebrated, the fair haired eleven year old boy and the dark little girl being ceremoniously put to bed under a single coverlet.

This first meeting was to blossom into one of the greatest of medieval love stories, passing into the realm of legend and song. It was a love that developed almost imperceptibly from the seed of these childish beginnings and grew into a tree so strong, supple and enduring, that it was spoken of long after both had died. Indeed this love, in later years, linked Louis with the sanctity of his wife, so that he too was venerated as a saint in parts of his kingdom.

A child can love; and Elizabeth, deprived of native land

and blood ties, was to pour the wealth of love latent within her upon this boy. She loved with all the ardour and tenderness of a devotion that never soured, because both knew how to keep it fresh, pure and rooted in God.

The world of the thirteenth century

Upon your walls, O Jerusalem, I have posted sentinels; all day and all night they shall never be silent. You who remind the Lord, take no rest until he establishes Jerusalem and makes it renowned throughout the earth.
Is. 62:6,7

Jesus said: 'There is still one thing lacking. Sell all you own and distribute the money to the poor, and you will have treasure in heaven; then come, follow me.'
Lk. 18:22

Elizabeth's world was a world in flux. Just as she herself journeyed from Hungary to Thuringia in her youth, so the world around her was on the move, physically and spiritually.

It was the era of the Crusades and men everywhere were being summoned to arms to conquer and defend the Holy Places. Her father-in-law had already been on a Crusade, her father was to participate in one soon, and later her husband likewise.

The twelfth century, following on the conquest of Jerusalem by Godfrey de Bouillon in 1091, had seen the rise of new Orders like the Knights Templar, the Knights Hospitaller, and latterly the Teutonic Knights (of which one of Elizabeth's brothers-in-law would one day be the Grand Master). These military Orders, dedicated to the defence of the Holy Land, promulgated the idea of knighthood as a sacred vocation.

Concomitantly the position of women changed. With so many men abroad they had to find new ways to employ their time, and with husbands and sons, fathers and lovers absent, they gradually developed a new independence. Then there was the ideal of romantic love associated with knighthood: women were set on pedestals worshipped from afar. They were living images of the Virgin Mary, the woman *par excellence*, divorced from the realities of sex. Like the ever present thought of the far Jerusalem, they were considered worthy of a lifetime's devotion even when that devotion promised no conquest, no physical consummation. Marriage was a contractual arrangement, a matter of duty and begetting legitimate heirs; for love, sexual fulfilment and marriage to coincide was

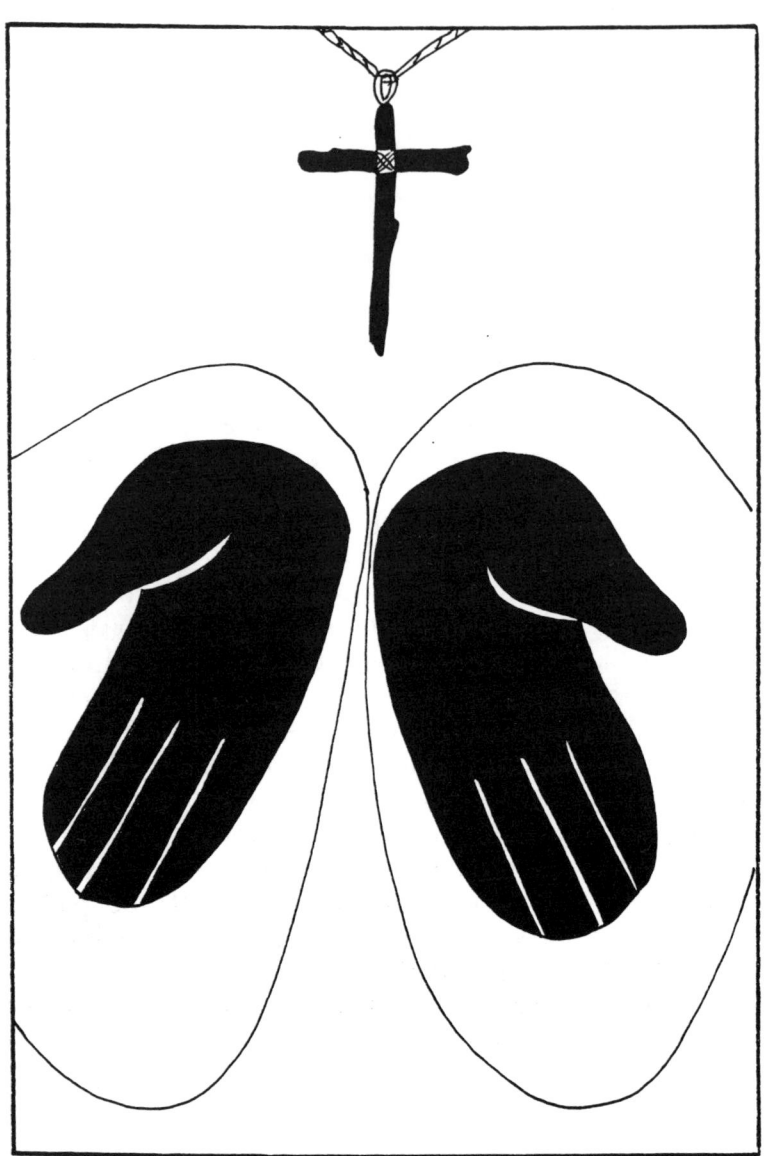

extremely unusual. A woman was either worshipped or 'used', and being a wife and mother was not necessarily related to either.

The mobility of the Crusades also opened up new travel routes with the East; silks, spices, beads, jewels, rich brocades were carried northwards from the Orient. A merchant class arose dealing with money, rather than bartering goods which had been the usual form of trade. High birth was not so important to these *nouveaux riches*. They could purchase all the trappings of the landed nobility without a hereditary pedigree; even knighthood for their sons was within reach.

As for the common people, they were the ones who suffered most, as always, in times of war and social upheaval. When petty princes were not trampling their lands, hoping for some minor extension of their property, and leaving a trail of rape, pillage and burnt crops, they were prey to crusading knights bribing them to 'take the cross' as part of a Christian fighting force.

When in desperation the poor left the land they had worked for generations and descended on the fast growing cities, hoping for employment and a share of their wealth, they found themselves in an even more precarious position. They were found labouring without rest in the great houses of merchants, dyeing cloth, breathing in noxious fumes from fires and vats, foraging in the gutters for scraps of food. Totally disoriented, they were an easy prey to diseases carried back from the East, hitherto unknown in Europe and therefore untreatable. If the afflicted were fortunate enough to obtain a hospital place, they found themselves laid beside pallets holding other wretched inmates displaying the worst kind of open sores, leprosy, fevers and plagues.

In the midst of these upheavals the Church was losing her influence over the masses. She had remained bound to a feudal way of life and was unprepared for the growth of the cities with their stress on a new equality and money based economy. Large monastic institutions seemed tied to the nobility and the land. Who would care for and instruct the indigent poor of the cities? Who would remind them that there was a God who cared about them in their misery? They knew only an elaborate Latin liturgy, fine vestments and the trappings of abbatial splendour. Could there possibly be a God who was close, compassionate?

The dominant religious figure of the thirteenth century was Francis of Assisi, who was born in 1181. His father was a wealthy cloth merchant who could afford to purchase for his son the accoutrements of knighthood as well as gifting him with unlimited amounts of money, ensuring that he was a welcome companion and reveller among his peers. Francis enjoyed all that his family provided, leading the youth of Assisi in feasting and revelry, arraying himself in gorgeous clothes and fine furs.

Then, at the age of twenty, Francis was taken prisoner durHeg a campaign against Perugia. The city states were continually at war and it was considered a matter of honour to defend the liberty of one's own commune. This time Assisi was defeated and Francis confined to prison for a while. The enforced solitude made him ponder on his way of life and his future, and he returned to Assisi a changed man. No longer could games and parties and tourneys satisfy him. In the midst of feasts he would become dreamy and abstracted. His companions were puzzled. What had happened to the young man who had been until recently the king of their revels?

However, Francis gathered his scattered wits once more, and when he had regained his health sufficiently he decided on a knightly career. His father, Pietro Bernadone, supplied him with a magnificent outfit, but on the way to enlist he had a dream. In the dream a voice asked him, 'Is it better to serve the Master or the servant?' 'The Master, of course,' answered Francis. 'Then why serve the servant?' asked the mysterious interrogator. Francis then realised that it was the Lord who was speaking to him. 'Lord, what will you have me do?' he asked. 'Go home. There you will be told what to do.' Francis turned his horse round and rode back in the direction from which he had come.

Back in Assisi, Francis waited for his future to unfold. He made a pilgrimage to Rome and there changed clothes with a beggar, that he might experience at first hand what it felt like to be indigent. Gradually poverty was becoming an ideal for him, something desirable in itself because chosen by the Son of God. Ftancis began to love and espouse poverty as his 'lady'. It was a complete *volte face* after his frivolous youth.

Francis next began to give time to God. He would go off to be silent in the wooded environs of Assisi, pondering and praying over the life of Christ. The watershed came when he conquered his fastidiousness and kissed a leper. He realised then, existentially, that Christ was present in the persons of the poor and destitute. Loving poverty, then, meant choosing a life of identification with the least, the *minores*, of society.

In the year 1207, the year in which Elizabeth was born, while praying in the little church of St. Damien, Francis seemed to hear the Crucifix speaking to him with the words 'Rebuild my church, Francis.' At first he took the words literally and began rebuilding churches that were in ruins, collecting stones, organising the fetching and carrying of timber and supplies. But in doing these basic tasks it dawned on him that he was really being summoned to inaugurate a spiritual rebuilding through a radical following of the Gospel.

Today we have so assimilated the Franciscan ideal into our Christian heritage that it does not cause the sense of shock and outrage that it once did. Imitate Christ literally? Have nowhere to lay one's head? Leave all to live the life of an itinerant preacher? Other reform movements had tried and failed in such a radical venture because their proponents had become bitter and vengeful against the rich, the landowners, the nobility and the institutional church. Francis instead took the path not of criticism, but of lived imitation. He showed that it could be done, and it could be done with love, not condemnation.

Pietro Bernadone was completely nonplussed. The hopes for the future of his business lay with his son. He had given Francis everything to make him successful and happy, and now Pietro's plans were in ruins and Francis a laughing-stock. When Francis sold a bale of valuable cloth to pay for building supplies, Pietro decided his son must appear before the bishop and be admonished to show proper respect for his parents. Poor father! One cannot help but feel sorry for the bewildered man.

The citizens duly gathered in the town square to witness the outcome of the confrontation. Before them all Francis removed his clothing and stood stark naked before his compatriots, saying that he returned everything to his father including the very clothes he was wearing. 'Henceforth I will no longer call Pietro Bernadone my father; I will say only "Our Father who art in heaven".'

The break was now complete. The bishop took Francis under his protection as a man dedicated to religion, but apart from that Francis was now classless, moneyless, without family ties and without status. He left the city wearing only a rough tunic, patched and tattered, a rope holding it together round his waist.

From these strange beginnings people came to join Francis in their hundreds, later in their thousands. His followers spread over Europe as 'lesser brothers'. Itinerant preachers, they eschewed large monasteries as their residences. Instead they bedded down in hovels in the towns among the very poor, or they constructed rude huts in the countryside. They begged their food, working with their hands at any task they could. It was a life of Gospel poverty close to nature, close to ordinary people.

Francis had a gift of making the neglected, the oppressed, the lepers, the outcasts of society feel that they mattered. His ideals spread to women under the direction of St. Clare and then to myriad layfolk for whom he wrote a simple Rule. Not all could live as friars or Poor Ladies, but that need be no bar to the full embracing of the Gospel.

Francis knew how to make religion real. He could speak of God in a way that could be understood by the masses. He made the first Christmas crib, he organised pilgrimages, he preached Christ as the Poor One present among us in crib, cross and Eucharist: a God who wanted to be truly incarnate in daily life, however humble.

On a spiritual level Francis revealed the ultimate meaning of poverty: reliance on God alone for grace and salvation. All comes from God. We have nothing we can call our own; before God we are all beggars. Conformity to Christ is therefore to choose what he chose: poverty, abjection, service of others, the cross. It means eschewing fame and praise and the desire for human esteem. We cannot earn favour or buy grace. Before God all are of equal worth.

Consciousness of his own wretchedness opened Francis to the wonder of salvation, freely offered to all in Christ. Having nothing, relying on Providence, opens one to love, to freedom, to grateful acceptance and joy.

With all this, it can be that people overlook the deep spirit of penance in Franciscan spirituality, but it is certainly present. The Third Order, originally for lay people, was known as the Order of Penance, and the Poor Ladies were known for their very penitential way of life.

Franciscanism is not a nature-based spirituality, a spirituality primarily concerned with birds, animals and the care of the environment. It is Incarnational in its fullest sense. God has come to us in the flesh and he wants to live again in our own flesh. This means we meet him in the flesh in others, especially in the neediest and poorest of our brothers and sisters. But this encounter with the other must mean the death of our selfishness, possessiveness, desire to dominate and control.

Nature is beautiful because it shares the beauty of Christ and is created by the Father. It is free and can be appreciated by rich and poor alike. It is because the poor have less possibility of possessing and manipulating nature that they are more open to joy. Penance and joy are two sides of the same coin: trust in providence and self-abasement.

The Franciscan path to holiness is not easy, but it is basically simple. Its appeal lies in its directness of approach and its personal devotion to Christ. Spiritual poverty hollows out the soul so that there is space made for God. He alone fills the horizon and is present in all whom we meet and serve throughout the day.

In due course we shall see how Francis influenced Elizabeth and how she found in him a kindred spirit. Miles separated them, their social status differed as well as their vocational bias, Elizabeth being a nobly born woman and Francis a poor, wandering preacher. But all this was peripheral to their shared vision and ideal. It was Francis who convinced Elizabeth that holiness was for her, just as she was; and his example was the sustaining support of her last years when she truly attained the heights of sanctity.

At this point in our story, when Elizabeth travelled to Thuringia as a four year old child, Francis' Order was growing and his ideals beginning to penetrate all levels of society. It was impossible that Elizabeth, with her passionate nature which knew no half measures, should not find in him a guide and friend. Her own life's journey, outwardly so different, was yet interiorly consumed with similar desires. She dreamed as she grew older of being one with Christ the Lord who was the living reality of her life from childhood onwards. And why not? The Franciscan ideal affirms in practice that before God differences of race, class and social standing are irrelevant. Before God all are poor and needy, and the key to discovering the living Lord lies in the service of the least of our brothers and sisters.

The growing years

Do not press me to leave you or to turn back from following you!
Where you go, I will go;
Where you lodge, I will lodge; your people shall be my people,
and your God, my God,
Where you die, I will die. There will I be buried.
May the Lord do thus and so to me, and more as well if even
death parts me from you.
Ruth 1:16-17

    The four year old Elizabeth was soon installed as a member of the family in the Wartburg castle, Hermann's principal residence.

    It was a fine stone fortress, built on the summit of a rock and surrounded by forested slopes for which Thuringia was famed. Firs and beech trees abounded, their magnificent foliage and variegated greens giving to the mountain a rich, verdant appearance. Below, the town of Eisenach throbbed with life and movement as prelates, knights, visiting dignitaries and an array of princes, margraves, landgraves, counts and their retinues made their way to the Wartburg to discuss politics, war and the current changing fortunes of the Holy Roman Empire. So much was the Wartburg to become synonymous with German culture and magnificence that Hitler chose it as the place where Nazi youth gathered to celebrate the Thousand Year Reich.

    When Elizabeth arrived at the Wartburg it was still in the process of being developed beyond its fortress-like exterior into a residence that would express Hermann's newly acquired wealth and position. The walls, thick and strong, enclosed a paved courtyard where jousting and tournaments took place. There was a large hall hung with silk and tapestries for warmth. There were well-appointed stables and kitchens, for Hermann was renowned for his hospitality. He entertained lavishly, never stinting himself for the sake of his guests. Wine was plentiful, coming to the table pressed from his own locally grown grapes. There were roasted meats, poultry, vegetables, honeyed confections, fruit. These were consumed in

great quantities while jongleurs and troubadours sang of love and heroic exploits to the revellers.

One of the most famous of the minnesingers, Walter von der Vogelweide, commented: "I advise anyone who has any ear trouble to stay away from the court of Thuringia, for if he goes there he will surely become deaf. . . . . I joined in the noise until I could stand it no longer. One group leaves, another enters, night and day.

In this lively, stimulating and cultured household, Elizabeth was assigned to the *kemenate* (the room with a hearth) reserved for the use of the women and children, although Hermann also took meals there with his family when he was at home, But it was a rare occasion when he was not entertaining in his usual fashion.

Sophia, who presided over the woman's quarters, was Hermann's second wife. He already had two married daughters by his first wife and six children by Sophia, two girls and four boys. The eldest, Irmingard, already absent when Elizabeth came to Wartburg, was the bride of Henry of Anhalt. Then came the boys, Louis, Hermann, Henry Raspe and Conrad.

The two eldest boys, lads of ten and eleven, were no longer confined to the *kemenate*; they were acquiring the manners of future knighthood and often accompanied their father on his journeys. Their time was spent in pursuits considered necessary for young men who had an assured place in society. They wrestled and jousted with their peers, learned to ride and to hunt, were instructed in the intricacies of courtly behaviour and the martial arts. Henry Raspe and Conrad, seven and five respectively, still shared the women's room, while Agnes, Elizabeth's own age, was her constant companion and playmate.

However, Agnes and Elizabeth were not left entirely to their own devices, and a sort of rivalry seems to have been present between them. Each had her own maids in waiting and a circle of other children considered socially suitable companions. A young German girl, Guda, was assigned to be Elizabeth's personal confidante, and from her testimony we can learn something of the saint's childhood. In her teenage years,

Guda was joined by Ysentrude, a young widow. These two always remained faithful to their Hungarian mistress, who they counted as being their dearest friend. They lived with her at the Wartburg, shared her growing up years, her experience as wife and mother, and finally her consecration to God as a Franciscan sister.

It has been said that 'no man is a hero to his valet', or concommitantly, 'no woman is a heroine to her maids', but Elizabeth inspired in those close to her a deep loyalty. She had the happy knack of accepting all as her equals. She refrained from anything, quite unselfconsciously, that might have implied that she despised others who did not share her royal birth and position.

We can presume that Elizabeth's education was consonant with that given to other young women of her age and class. She learned how to sew and embroider, and how to cultivate herbs and blend them into medicinal potions, for the mistress of a great household was supposed to take an interest in the health and general wellbeing of those around her.

Under the tuition of the two Hungarian priests in exile Elizabeth would have learned to read, and become familiar with the history of the Hungarian nation and its links with Thuringia, as well as retaining a working knowledge of her mother tongue. A bilingual child has a great advantage because of the breadth of knowledge and culture available to one who is fluent in two languages, but it can also induce a feeling of not belonging completely to either world. Perhaps Elizabeth felt this ambivalence and so turned Godwards to find her deepest identity as a Christian, a daughter of God, rather than as a Hungarian princess betrothed to the heir of Thuringia.

As she matured, Elizabeth mastered the duties that would be hers as a married woman. She learned about presiding at banquets and the range of foods she would be expected to offer her guests. There were lessons in the art of conversation, in the intricacies of dress and fashion: not formal lessons necessarily, but the knowledge that is imbibed unconsciously from significant adults in a young person's life and is easily absorbed by those with a quick mind, eager to please. Dancing, music and poetry were required accomplishments, as were some knowledge of falconry and horseriding. Elizabeth proved to be an excellent horsewoman who later enjoyed accompanying her husband on his travels.

And what of religion? The future saint sounds as if she would be a girl thoroughly imbued with the arrogance so often found in those possessing privilege and wealth. Hence it is surprising to discover that with Elizabeth her natural womanhood seems to have developed without deviance. She was forthright, unspoiled, blessed with a disposition that was obliging and sunny. She never decried her upbringing or turned her back on the rich cultural and social life that surrounded her. She was what she was, a girl of her own time engaged to a boy she was growing to love. Elizabeth had no hankering for the convent, no unfulfilled yearning for the discipline and dedication of a nun. But religion was woven into the fabric of her being. It was the atmosphere she breathed and of which she was most conscious even amid all the distractions of the court. To be sure, Christian Europe expected all its rulers to be conversant with common prayers and to attend Mass on Sundays at least, and often daily: that was considered only right and customary. It was taken for granted that priests were part of every noble household and would administer the private chapels found in any castle or palace of note. The Wartburg had its own chapel, with a new one in process of construction when Elizabeth was a child. Even before being able to read, Elizabeth would have marvelled at the rich illuminations in her mother-in-law's prayer book. Sophia was considered a devout woman and her Book of Hours was a small masterpiece of the illuminator's art.

But there is devotion and devotion. Sophia and Agnes, for all their piety, were careful to keep within the bounds of what was considered good taste in their religious practices. Elizabeth on the other hand was extravagant and vital in her response from the first. All that had to do with Christ and his Church awakened echoes in her childish heart. She was 'naturally' religious. For her the normal conventions did not apply. Any perfunctory performance of her Christian duties was simply not for her.

The living Christ was Elizabeth's first love. Devotion to

him was not merely a social obligation, one among many others that filled her days. Guda speaks of Elizabeth finding opportunities in her games to lead her companions by way of the chapel so that she could make a quick visit; of promising a Hail Mary should she win at hide and seek; of prostrating herself on the floor, ostensibly to compare the strength of her body with others of her age, but in reality using this gesture as a sign of adoration: small things that could have been the result of youthful enthusiasm soon to fade. It is the life that developed from these tiny shoots and bore the fruit of a mature devotion that proved the sincerity of these first acts of love.

Legend speaks of Sophia and Agnes having a settled dislike of Elizabeth. Evidence points rather to their kindness and care for the little exile in their household. But she was considered 'strange', no doubt about it, and she had to bear a certain amount of motherly and sisterly disapproval when it came to her religious practices. It was all too much for the persons whose piety kept within the bounds of conventional good taste. God was all very well so long as he was kept in his proper place!

So the early years at the Wartburg passed. Elizabeth seems to have had a relatively normal and happy childhood; and her basic character was taking shape in such a way that her whole life seems to have one unbroken line of loving dedication. Even though outward circumstances might change, the inner direction was constant. She was like an arrow speeding straight to its sure and ultimate destination.

The flowering of love

Set me as a seal upon your heart, as a seal upon your arm,
for love is strong as death,
passion fierce as the grave,
Its flashes are flashes of fire, a raging flame.
Many waters cannot quench love, neither can floods drown it.
S. S. 8:6, 7

While Elizabeth was receiving her own early education in the *kemenate* as a future wife and mother, Louis was pursuing his path to knighthood, being initiated gradually by his father into the affairs of government. Contact between the betrothed pair was sporadic but always tender and courteous. They called one another 'dear brother', 'dear sister', as their greatest and most intimate endearment all through their lives. They were destined for a life together from childhood and they acted accordingly.

At what point this arranged match passed from childish affection into the area of adult and deep love we cannot say. Most likely it was something that grew imperceptibly while the years of betrothal passed, until it was a shining bond welding two hearts into one.

Elizabeth, far from home and native land, poured upon Louis all the pent up ardour of her passionate temperament. However, she never delegated to him the responsibility she felt for her own actions and conscience. She was uniquely herself. Louis had the privileged love of a woman who knew her own mind and did not expect her husband to define the perimeter of her life and interests.

With Elizabeth's growing love for Christ and for her future husband, went a marked attraction to the poor. The Wartburg had its share of beggars, cripples, wanderers, those disfigured by disease and the horrible scars of war and pestilence. Elizabeth was not insensitive to the fact that her own situation was very different from theirs. She was naturally drawn to the less fortunate, compassionately desiring to do whatever she could to alleviate their sufferings.

Any repugnance Elizabeth may have felt at the sight and

touch of running sores, gangrene, decay, pus, blood and greenish discharge, was never displayed. She would go out to the sick at the castle gate carrying her carefully prepared herbal ointments and potions. 'She laughed, was pleasant and light hearted' as Guda testified, never showing disgust. She sympathetically washed and tended the sick with whatever means she had at her disposal, always with a smile upon her lips. Elizabeth was gifted with the attributes of what might be termed 'the born nurse'.

That gaiety, which permeated any dealings with those suffering even from the most horrible maladies, was not forced. It arose spontaneously from the depths of her heart. It was a case of grace perfecting nature, rather than Elizabeth channeling her behaviour in a direction alien to her temperament and inclinations.

We could be tempted to pause here and exclaim, 'This child is unnatural!' But is she really? Is it not *we* who are unnatural in our aversion towards those who should arouse in us sentiments of pity? Is it not a gift from God, given to us all, when we see a young girl growing up with such seemingly unforced integrity, selflessly overcoming the restraints of convention in her search for truth and love?

Maybe we are jealous, unconsciously perhaps, when we see a child of grace, one of ourselves, reflecting what human nature can be at its best. Do we not rather identify with the people who found Elizabeth altogether 'too much'. We would certainly like to have her gifts if they were ours. But unlike her we might be unwilling to pay the price demanded of one so gifted, as we shall see later. If we could simply accept her as one given by God to show one aspect of God's unbounded love and compassion we might attain to some glimmer of the truth.

While Elizabeth was a religious child who developed into a loving girl and devout young woman, she was unlike many pious young people who betray in their maturity a strained and forced personality which disapproves of joy and is hampered by fear and guilt. On the contrary Elizabeth's vital forces were not restricted. Hers was no stifling, hothouse piety. Her virtue had strong, natural roots which thrust deep into her burgeoning womanhood. She loved Christ, she loved Louis, she loved the poor, she loved her friends and companions. Life was good, and her awakening sexuality was not wrenched out of shape by false shame or the fear of future childbearing.

Elizabeth's growing years, however, were not unmarred. There were the inevitable misunderstandings generated by those who found her forthright and spontaneous approach to life unpalatable. And there were major tragedies of a personal order. Elizabeth's mother was murdered when her daughter was six years old, What she knew of the circumstances attendant on that death we can only conjecture, but she would at least have been aware that the woman who had endowed her so richly for the journey to Thuringia was now cold in her grave many miles away. The silver bath was now a continual reminder of the one she would never see again.

Hermann, the Landgrave's second son, also died during Elizabeth's girlhood. He was Louis' closest companion and her own foster brother. The Landgrave Hermann died a year later. Ftom the chronicles of the time it appears that he sank into a deep depression which moved inexorably into insanity. The spectacle of the mad ruler who had maintained his court in such splendour during his time of power and glory cast a cloud over the whole country. The court was in disarray as the disease progressed. Sophia thought it was due to Hermann's bad consience for he was a formidable enemy to those he hated. When he died she retired to a Cistercian convent to pray continually for his soul.

Throughout these sorrows Elizabeth had to keep a brave exterior. It also meant that she was closer to Louis who became her friend and comforter as she his. He had to assume the powers of succession when he was only sixteen, thus Elizabeth's position at court became more prominent. She had to adjust to the role of Landgravine when barely ten.

At eighteen Louis officially attained knighthood. Elizabeth, now eleven and considered a young woman, watched as her fiancé, dressed in white with a red cross emblazoned on his surcoat, took the feudal oath. He spent the previous night of vigil in prayer before the altar, intending to take his knighthood seriously as a vocation in its own right.

After the ceremony there was much feasting and jousting,

with visitors and guests swelling the numbers who rejoiced with the affianced couple on this great occasion. Of the love that bound these two together there could be no doubt. They were as two plants intertwined at the roots to form one glorious bloom. It was no merely 'supernatural' love, if by that we mean that they saw only God in one another and went ahead with their engagement from a sense of duty to their people and kingdom, but without much personal emotion. No, this love, especially on Elizabeth's side, was passionate and absorbing, while being totally consonant with her religious aspirations and her devotion to Christ.

At some point there seems to have been a question of the engagement being broken off, thus allowing Louis to make a better political alliance. By this time Elizabeth's father was losing influence in Europe. His misrule made his daughter a less desirable acquisition than was formerly the case when the betrothal was first entered into. It was suggested that Elizabeth might return to Hungary or, if she wished, enter a convent.

Helplessly Elizabeth awaited a decision while voicing her preference for Louis. The life of an enclosed nun held no attraction for her active, charitable temperament. The thought of being put once more on the marriage market for the highest bidder was also abhorrent. Fortunately Louis knew his own mind and his own rights. He and Elizabeth were affianced and he was determined they should stay that way.

Whenever Louis returned from a journey he would miss no opportunity of bringing something with him as a small love token for the woman of his choice. This was a time when knights who travelled were expected to have romantic attachments to ideal women at various castles, as well as liasons to fulfil their sexual needs. A woman was often provided as bed companion as a matter of course. Louis rejected all pressure in this area of his life, determined to be faithful to Elizabeth alone.

One day Elizabeth, fearful for her future, asked a friendly knight to obtain a love token for her from Louis as a symbol of his fidelity. Louis immediately sent a beautiful mirror with a glass on one side and on the reverse side a finely wrought crucifix. Elizabeth rejoiced, Louis had understood her perfectly!

In 1221 when Louis was twenty one and Elzabeth fourteen they were married. He was upright, pure, respectful, tender, wanting to rule justly and well. She was physically and spiritually attractive in every way. And so their vows were consummated by union. The following spring the young fifteen year old bride presented Louis with a son, Hermann. Louis was not present when the child was born as he was away on business. He immediately rewarded the messenger who had brought the news and decreed public rejoicing at the event: the inheritance was secure!

Louis and Elizabeth then undertook a journey to Hungary to visit King Andrew and his second wife, Yolande. Elizabeth rode much of the way on horseback, secure in her new wifely status. Together the couple enjoyed the celebrations which were organised by the Hungarian court in their honour. The banquets and entertainments were devised to assure Louis that his father-in-law was not a man of little account despite any tales that may have made their way to Thuringia. Also, Elizabeth met her father once more after an absence of eleven years. They must have been strangers to one another by now and most likely felt unable to touch on the sensitive subject of the murdered former queen.

Béla, Elizabeth's brother, himself married, was proving a popular heir-apparent. But Elizabeth's homeland was now Thuringia. She looked forward to returning and taking her rightful place beside her husband as Landgravine. She hoped for a life full of shared happiness and mutual support, while the child of their love, Hermann, grew strong aad was joined by other brothers and sisters.

While the outlook was propitious, Louis of course saw things in a wider perspective. He was a prince and ruler with lands to govern and extend by astute bargaining and possible warfare. But together he and Elizabeth would prosper. Few of his contemporaries had a wife such as the one who shared his bed and graced his banquets.

No longer children, Louis and Elizabeth, despite their youth, were adults in an adult world. Life was before them and they would face it together.

Growth in maturity

Like the sun rising in the heights of the Lord, so is the beauty of a good wife in her well-ordered home. Like the shining lamp on the holy lampstand, so is a beautiful face on a stately figure.
Sir. 26:16-17

Adulthood is about choices and the tensions that accompany limitations gladly accepted and worked through. One choice may seem to exclude others, but in reality a way has to be found whereby a balance can be maintained between various commitments and roles. The child can afford to be natural and spontaneous; responsibilities are part of adult development. These set up tensions in a life, for they must be reconciled with reality in all its manifestations.

A married person for example must balance the demands of spouse and children against the necessity of work and the demands incumbent upon making a living. Neither can married love be such that, for safety's sake, all other relationships are excluded.

At one time the pendulum may swing too far one way so that reponsibilities are neglected at work because one enjoys family life so much. If this happens, then those who are relying on a job being completed will complain, with good reason. Or so much time can be devoted to social success or career climbing that spouse and children are overlooked. An apostolic religious has to balance the demands of pressing service to those in need with the attraction to prayer, silence and the demands of a community life under vows. At one time one will predominate, then the pendulum must swing the other way if the balance is to be rectified.

We usually find it easier to cut tensions than to live with them and work through them. The pressure and stress contained in balancing choices is never easy and must be continually adjusted as circumstances change. The married may find it easier to devote all their time to either family or career over everything else. The religious may neglect prayer and immerse him or herself in social concern. Conversely, if prayer remains the dominant attraction then the needy who

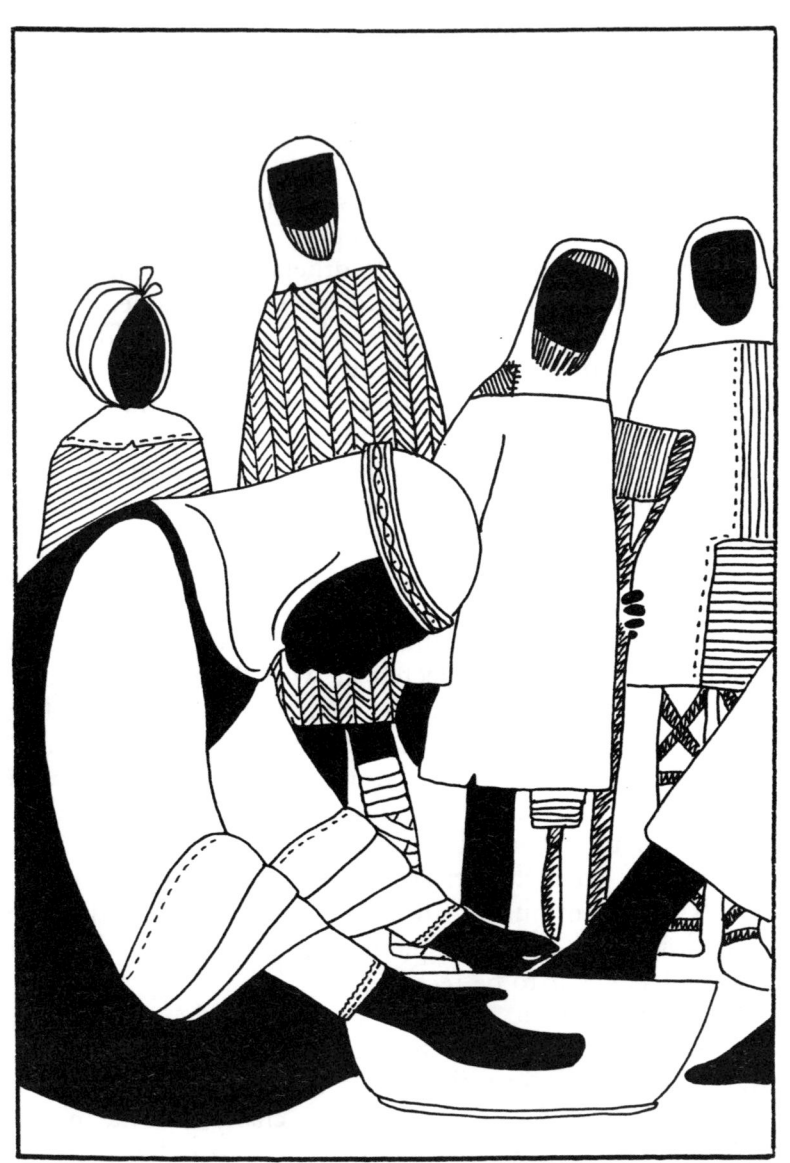

clamour for attention will be treated as an obstruction to 'real' devotion, instead of being recognised as an indispensable part of Christian self-giving.

Elizabeth likewise was faced with choices when as a woman she was confronted with the three great loves of her life; love for Christ, love for her husband and love for the poor. She knew that Christ must have first claim, that was obvious, but she could not spurn the husband she loved under pretext of prayer, nor could she neglect the poor who relied on her charity. All had to be combined in one synthesis. Indeed, because of Elizabeth's very state of life, love for Louis and service of the poor were incumbent upon her as expressions of her love for Christ.

On the natural level, it would have been understandable if a young wife, very much in love with her husband, let him become an idol. Or Elizabeth could lose herself in playing the 'lady bountiful' because it boosted her own image of herself as a charitable person. The years of her married life saw Elizabeth continually balancing these claims upon her attention and eventually finding a synthesis in her love for God which unified everything. The answers she found were uniquely hers and we have to see them as such. They are not models to imitate so much as they are pointers towards the kind of attitudes all must foster.

Elizabeth bore not only the responsibilities of a Christian wife and mother, she was also continually in the public eye as Landgravine. She presided over a household which comprised several royal residences and she managed the estates and their revenues during her husband's many absences. Louis was often away engaged on the Emperor's business. He was intent on extending his influence, and was therefore of necessity involved in all the political intrigues that accompany the possession of lands and power.

The first tension Elizabeth felt was one that touched her heart at its tenderest spot: her relationship with Louis. She struggled to neither smother her natural passion nor let it become a source of guilt (for to her it was God-given) but also not to let it swamp her completely. She saw that it would be wrong merely to become Louis' cipher and stifle her own personality.

The woman of the Old Testament was lauded as the one standing beside her husband. The valiant woman, the good wife, was a worker, a provider a tower of strength and conjugal chastity.

> A capable wife who can find?
> She is more precious than jewels.
> The heart of her husband trusts in her
> and he will have no lack of gain.
> She does him good and not harm all the days of her life.
> She seeks wool and flax and works with willing hands.
> She opens her hands to the needy and stretches out her hands to the poor,
> She is not afraid of snow for her household.
> Strength and dignity are her clothing and she laughs at the time to come.
> She opens her mouth with wisdom and the teaching of kindness is on her tongue.
> She looks well to the ways of her household and does not eat the bread of idleness.
>
> Prov. 31:10-13, 20, 21, 25, 26.

The strong woman was the ideal in Israel. On the other hand the Christian wife was often denigrated when compared with the virgin, one devoted wholly to the service of Christ and his kingdom.

Elizabeth's vocation was to meld these two into one within her own person. To be a mature Christian is in some sense to be the 'bride of Christ' whatever one's exterior circumstances. It is to put the love of Christ first not merely in theoretical conviction but in the tug of the heart and in practical life, To become such a woman, whether one is married or single, requires great purity of heart. Purity of heart is the goal of both ways to God. Indeed it is only in this purity that the Christian wife and mother is able to find the necessary strength to fulfil her vocation of ministering love. Ministering love is the essence of maternity and it has to flow out to embrace all who come within its orbit.

And so Elizabeth tried to balance her deep love for Louis

with her overriding love for Christ; to attain and sustain a purity of heart that neither stifled passion nor permitted her husband to take the place of God for her.

Several stories are told of her in this regard and there is obviously truth in them. Her retinue was as continually amazed at her emotional attachment to Louis in an era when passion and marriage were seldom paired, as they were nonplussed by her love for Christ when this was considered to be the domain of the consecrated virgin alone.

One day when Louis was to be bled, a common medical practice of the time, he held the customary feast and games that accompanied the bloodletting. The games were preceded by a High Mass in which the court appeared in its most glittering finery. Elizabeth and Louis were both present, he in his knightly apparel resplendent with jewels and precious metal. At the elevation of the Host Elizabeth raised her eyes to adore, but instead her gaze fell on her husband who was looking so splendid. Forgetting the Host she feasted her eyes on her lover. Almost immediately, remorse overcame her. How could she have turned from the Creator to the creature at such a sacred moment? She remained after Mass weeping, prostrate with genuine sorrow.

Louis noticed Elizabeth's absence from the feast that followed. When he discovered the reason for it he went out personally to persuade her to come in. But she was so distressed he had eventually to withdraw, excusing her absence to his guests with kindness.

At night also, Elizabeth would rise to pray secretly; even so she would do it clasping the hand of the sleeping Louis. It was as if her happiness were too great. She could not contain it but she did not want to deprive God of all her attention during those sacred hours of darkness. Lest she should sleep uninterruptedly Elizabeth had the faithful Guda or Ysentrude wake her by tugging at her foot, a silent signal that it was time to pray.

Apparently one night Louis' foot had moved itself to Elizabeth's side of the bed and it was he who was awakened by the maid's tug. He was momentarily angry at the familiarity but when he discovered the mistake he laughed as loud as the rest of them. No doubt he was much more aware of Elizabeth's custom than he let on. But the nights they spent together must have been generally fewer than both desired, as records show that for at least half of their married life Louis was away on campaigns or business. All the more reason then, to admire Elizabeth's resolve not to enjoy her husband's presence without reference to God, the source of her bliss.

When Louis was away Elizabeth laid aside her finery and dressed as a widow to show her bereaved state. She devoted herself then to the service of the poor and to humble work such as spinning and weaving. But when she heard that Louis was returning home a horse would be saddled for her and she would gallop out to meet him. Then, before the hard-bitten soldiers, she would throw herself into his arms, 'covering his mouth with a thousand kisses', as the ancient chronicler reported, almost with a hint of disapproval at such conduct.

When her husband was in residence Elizabeth would wear her finest dresses, furs and silks in order that her presence might bring him joy and honour in the eyes of the court. She wanted to ensure that nothing on her part should tempt him to infidelity. This could have been the case had she shown herself to be a prude, or one who despised the gifts of a husband who loved to see his wife adorned in a manner befitting her royal rank.

It is obvious from these stories of her contemporaries, even allowing for the excesses of hagiography, that between Louis and Elizabeth there was mutual respect and trust. He had his kingdom to govern; she, on the other hand, did not just live in his shadow: she was permitted to make her own choices, live her own life. She used the time given her for the service of the poor and sick, coupled with the building and overseeing of a hospital. She ran her household with diligent application and saw to the distribution of money when required. Louis had no cause to be ashamed of his wife when dignitaries visited or festivities were arranged.

Elizabeth's other great love beside Christ and Louis was her love for the poor: a devotion to the poor that from childhood had seemed to come naturally and was totally unforced. But service to the poor alone could not satisfy her. She began by simplifying her dress as an outward symbol of interior identification.

The costume of Elizabeth's peers was elaborate; a gown with a train pulled tightly in at the waist, a cloak of rich material with cord and clasp, a head covering of linen or gauze passing under the chin and covering most of the hair which was parted in the middle and worn high at the back. Over the headress, a flat round cap of starched linen was fixed, with a veil attached for princesses and young girls. The rich wore elaborately embroidered tunics, the sleeves of the surcoat often being detachable. These sleeves swept the ground at the wrist and were tight fitting at the armhole. Often the fit was so close the sleeves had to be sewn into place each time the garment was put on.

Elizabeth seems to have had a real aversion to these rich sleeves which proclaimed one's rank and were crafted from the most precious cloth such as silver brocade or velvet. She resolved never to wear them before Mass and persuaded her maids to adopt the same practice. Likewise she wanted those in her retinue to eschew at least some object of finery out of love for God. She herself liked to remove her jewellery and other adornments before Mass and humbly lower her veil at the Consecration.

One of the most famous episodes of Elizabeth's life took place in the Church of St. Catherine at Eisenach, where Sophia and Agnes were attending Mass in splendid attire and Elizabeth, who was acompanying them, wore a jewelled coronet. On seeing the image of Christ thorn-crowned and crucified she removed her own circlet, saying she did not think it a fitting adornment for one who follow a crucified Saviour.

This gesture hardly endeared her to others who thought it altogether too ostentatious. But to Elizabeth it was sincere. She much preferred simplicity and after childbirth would go for her churching garbed as a poor peasant. She said that this was how Our Lady had taken Jesus to the Temple. It is also possible that in childbearing Elizabeth identified herself most humanly with her womanhood and not her rank. She was a mother three times over, her eldest child being her son Hermann, then came Sophia, named for her mother-in-law, and lastly Gertrude, born just after Louis' death.

When Elizabeth served the poor she wanted to do it in person and not through intermediaries. She would tend even the worst cases of sores and fevers 'with her own hands', which is the constant refrain of those who testified to her life. She showed no sign of disgust but always smiled as though it were she who was the privileged one. She saw each person with different needs, each one as needing personal care.

When it came to the distribution of alms, Elizabeth knew no bounds. While Louis was away a famine devastated the countryside and Elizabeth emptied the reserves stored for the court and distributed everything to the needy. When Louis' courtiers brought this imprudent behaviour to his notice on his return he defended his wife's actions with his customary vigour. Let her give as she thought fit, not as human prudence dictated. What Louis himself thought of the hordes of beggars and outcasts who beseiged the castle looking for alms from his wife, is not recorded. However, the fact that he allowed Elizabeth a free hand both in her nursing and in her almsgiving is testimony enough.

With such a spiritual attraction to poverty and to the poor it can be no surprise that Elizabeth, on hearing about St. Francis, recognised a kindred spirit. She sent for Friars Minor to come to Thuringia and endowed them generously, choosing a Franciscan Confessor, Brother Rodeger, to direct her. It is said that Francis, apprised of Elizabeth's generosity to his friars, sent her his own cloak as a gift. In this she would clothe herself when she went to pray for any special intention. No fragment remains of this precious relic, so whether the incident should be relegated to the realm of legend is not clear, but it is a legend worthy of such great lovers as Francis, the poor man of Assisi, and Elizabeth, daughter of the King of Hungary. In fact, one of Francis' best friends, the Lady Jacoba, was also a rich woman, and he said that she understood him better than many who lived according to his Rule. On his deathbed he asked for her, and she arrived bringing the special sweetmeats he loved. Friendship and understanding are not confined to the usual boundaries that we like to place on ourselves and others.

One year before his death, Louis approved a new confessor

for his wife, one highly recommended for his austerity and orthodoxy, Conrad of Marburg. The very name is enough to send a shiver down the spine when we look at him in retrospect, but the fact remains that under Conrad's direction Elizabeth reached sanctity. God's ways are not our ways and to contemplate this gentle and joy-filled woman under the direction of such a grim priest seems incomprehensible.

Conrad was not a Franciscan but a secular priest noted for his penitential life and his fiery preaching. He eschewed all luxury for himself and was known to be recommended by the Pope himself as a man fittingly endowed and thus able to be entrusted with preaching the crusade as well as ferreting out heretics for punishment. Later Conrad exceeded all limits in his zeal against heretics and he was so hated that he was murdered, notwithstanding that he had been renowned as the confessor of the now canonised Elizabeth.

In 1226, when Conrad was recommended to Elizabeth he was, though austere, not tainted by the later excesses that have made his memory odious; rather he was noted for his perfection and love of poverty. When Louis suggested him to Elizabeth she took it as the will of God, making a vow of obedience to Conrad and later, under his auspices and with some solemnity, a vow to remain continent in the event of Louis' death. Elizabeth was to say that she could have vowed obedience to any bishop or abbot of her choice but she preferred Conrad in that he owned nothing and was a true mendicant.

This did not stop Elizabeth fearing the man whom she had given such power over her. His severity sometimes went as far as whipping and blows if she disobeyed, even inadvertently and in the slightest thing. For example, on one occasion she omitted attending one of Conrad's sermons and stayed at home to welcome her sister-in-law, Jutta; a welcome dictated by political expediency as much as politeness, since Louis and Jutta had only just been reconciled after a family feud relating to her inheritance. Elizabeth felt it was her duty to be present when Jutta arrived but Conrad was incensed. He refused to accept an apology and had Elizabeth and her maids dressed as penitents and whipped.

The most noteworthy obligation that Conrad imposed on Elizabeth under her vow of obedience to him was that of the *Speisegebot*. By it Elizabeth was to identify with her beloved poor in a most radical way: she was forbidden to avail herself of any food that might have been obtained by unjust means and this, not as a matter of charity but of plain justice. In any age, even our own, such a command would be well nigh impossible to carry out once a tender conscience was aroused. In Elizabeth's era it was unheard of, extravagant, and led the princess into such straits that many a time she sat starving before a full board at her husband's table. For how could she be sure that everything served had been justly obtained? Maybe the hunt had galloped over lands that were in another's possession; maybe the peasants had been deprived of their sustenance in paying rents to their Lord; maybe Church property had been devastated. Unless Elizabeth was absolutely sure of its provenance all food was forbidden.

If we tried to follow the same ruling today it would be as difficult for us as it was for Elizabeth. Many times she and her ladies had to subsist on small portions of bread before a table groaning under roast meats and honeyed desserts. Wine from her husband's own vineyards was all right, other drinks suspect. From her own resources, the money from her dower, Elizabeth did her best to purchase food that she knew was free from taint. It hurt her even more to see her ladies joining her in her self denial than it did to go without nourishment herself. But on days when she knew the food was lawful she would clap her hands with glee, giving vent to joyful laughter, eating and drinking with a glad heart and making up for the days of deprivation.

That Louis allowed this behaviour, which could be interpreted as at least a tacit criticism of his own way of life, proves how he venerated Elizabeth's conscience. Of course, in later years, when Elizabeth was a canonised saint, all this was taken as being part of her extraordinary holiness. At the time it could only be considered as an arrogance which she had abrogated to herself in order to teach a lesson to her elders and betters: people equally 'religious' but not so 'fanatical' !

It could not have been easy for Elizabeth to keep to the

course Conrad had set her. At the time we are speaking of she was but nineteen, a young mother who was devoted to her children and her husband, and was continually engaged in charitable activity. Her charity was becoming in every way the charity of the cross. It was based with growing intensity on a sacrificial love for Christ's poor, and a desire to be conformed to his image. This was borne out by hours of prayer and vigil as well as active, loving service to the needy.

The unimaginable anguish

Whatever gains I had, these I have come to regard as loss because of Christ. More than that, I regard everything as loss because of the surpassing value of knowing Christ Jesus my Lord. For his sake I have suffered the loss of everything and I regard it as rubbish in order that I may gain Christ and be found in him.
Phil. 4: 7-8

In 1227 Elizabeth was twenty years old and she and Louis had been married for six years. They already had two children and Elizabeth was pregnant with a third. This child, whether boy or girl, would be dedicated to God from infancy. It was the mutual decision of both parents, a thank-offering to God for the gift of their happy married life. In a time when marriage was so little valued apart from the political alliances it cemented among the nobility, Louis and Elizabeth were an example not only to the people of their realm but to the whole of European high society. Their influence was incalculable.

One day Louis was at home after one of his many sorties with the Emperor Frederick II. In a moment of intimacy he was sitting quietly while Elizabeth amused herself sorting through the odds and ends in his alms purse; a few coins, mementos, bits of wax. . . then her fingers alighted on a folded piece of material. She opened it and saw that it was the crusader's cross that was worn on the surcoat when a man left on a crusade. Louis must have taken the vow to liberate the Holy Land and this cross meant his departure was imminent. He had not told Elizabeth yet. Her gaze met his as she unwrapped the sign and held it in her palm. Louis' eyes confirmed the question in her gaze. The shock, coupled with her pregnancy, was too much for her and she fainted.

Elizabeth could have guessed that at some point Louis would join a crusade. It was expected of a Christian knight and was considered a sure pledge of salvation. Elizabeth, with her passionate attachment to Christ would long to see the Holy Places liberated from the infidel and open to pilgrims. But not at the cost of her beloved's life.

Elizabeth had given herself to the embrace of poverty, to

the ideals of St. Francis, to the care of lepers and other unfortunates. These fulfilled her longing to serve and she never thought that her behaviour in this regard was heroic. But her love for Louis was the great tie of her soul, the cutting of which she desperately resisted. For Louis, the crusader cross represented the high point of his knighthood, a glory that would be reflected on his wife if he returned victorious. But for Elizabeth it symbolised the supreme renunciation and she shrank from it. So many did not come home alive; as many died en route from disease as from wounds in battle. Pride in Louis, anguish and trepidation on her own account, mingled in her soul.

It was springtime in Thuringia, the first flowers were in bud. Did Elizabeth have a premonition that by the autumn of the same year, when the trees around the Wartburg were golden and scarlet, she would be a widow?

There was not much time to prepare for departure: the Emperor had already postponed one Crusade and was eager to get this one under way. Louis began to set his affairs in order.

To his brother, Henry Raspe, Louis left the guardianship of his son and the administration of the state; then he assembled his vassals to inform them of his departure and to ask for their loyal support during his absence. After this he travelled to the monasteries of men and women that he knew to beg their prayers. At Rheinshardsbrunn, his favourite cloister, he arrived at the hour of Compline when the Abbot was blessing the monks with holy water before they retired for the night. Louis spoke with each one in turn, but when it came to the children of the monastic school he took them up in his arms and kissed them. No doubt he thought wistfully of his own children and how they would miss his caresses; indeed they might well have forgotten their father by the time he returned.

St. John's day arrived, June 24th and Louis took leave of his domains and his family. The moment of separation loomed before wife and children. He blessed everyone present, once more recommended his wife and children to his brother and kissed his mother. Overcome with emotion he could not speak to the latter and they embraced in silence. Louis mounted his horse, accompanied by his knights and men at arms and the assembly broke into a hymn to sustain their courage. Elizabeth rode beside Louis, unable to tear herself away. Two days passed and they crossed the borders of Thuringia. Elizabeth was still with them.

But the hour had come for that last goodbye. Walter of Vargila, the royal cupbearer approached Louis. "The time has come to send our gracious lady back. It must needs be. " Louis controlled himself before his men: he was their leader and lord. He reached into his alms purse and drew out a ring on which the Lamb of God was engraved upon a sapphire, with this ring Louis sealed his most personal missives and he told his wife that she could believe any messenger bearing this token. Then they embraced for the last time, their love and longing pulsing through every fibre as their quivering bodies pressed together. Then Elizabeth turned her horse around and she and Louis rode in opposite directions.

On reaching the Wartburg Elizabeth removed her royal garments, exchanging them for those of a widow. Her charitable works continued but her prayers and vigils were prolonged. She would not rest from supplicating God for the safe return of her husband.

Meanwhile Louis and his men had traversed the Alps and reached the Adriatic Sea. When they reached Brindisi the crowded camp conditions, the torrid heat and tha lack of supplies caused a fever to take hold of the weakened troops and many died. The Emperor himself succumbed and while the first troops embarked for Palestine at the end of August he and Louis turned aside to Otranto, where they were to take leave of the young Empress Isabelle Yolande, heiress to the Kingdom of Jerusalem.

By this time, the fever had attacked Louis. He was weak with pain and vomiting but he went ashore to pay homage to the wife of his liege lord. Soon it became obvious to all that he would not recover. He received the last sacraments from the Patriarch of Jerusalem who was visiting Otranto and died on September 11th, without even having seen the country to which he was journeying with such chivalric hopes.

Louis' body was clad in full royal attire, wrapped in white sheets coated with wax,and buried with due honour. Then his knights, to fulfil their crusader vows, set sail for Palestine without the leader they had served so loyally. A messenger was sent to Elizabeth bearing the precious ring and the news of her husband's death.

Elizabeth was in the last stages of pregnancy, big with child and sad in her solitude. No one dared give her the tragic tidings until the child was born, a little girl, delivered on the twenty-ninth of September.

When it was judged that Elizabeth had recovered suffiently a small group of close friends and advisors approached the Wartburg. It was Sophia, her mother-in-law, who was chosen to say the fatal words, but Elizabeth must have guessed the purport of their visit when she saw the grave and tear-stained faces of her visitors. Still, she must hear the actual words, see the ring, let the words of comfort and pious reassurance wash over her frozen soul.

Gradually the truth penetrated the heart that was now pierced in a thousand places, the body that had exulted in Louis' embrace and had just born his child. In the face of this overwhelming grief she was just a poor woman, no 'saint' who could find edifying words to impress those around her who awaited her reaction.

Elizabeth clenched her fists upon her knees and lowered her head, A great cry burst from her that time has not been able to mitigate: '*Tot, tot sal mir nu alle wertliche froide unde ere si*': 'Dead, dead will be for me all happiness . . . ' She had lost the one who was her joy, her very life. In her blind reaction of grief she ran hither and thither in the room like a madwoman from one wall to another, pounding the stones with her fists and crying aloud in anguish 'May he who does not abandon the widow and orphan console me, O my God, my Jesus, console me, strengthen me in my weakness'. At last, in utter exhaustion, she sank to the floor her clenched fists raised above her head and resting against the wall. Gently her ladies dragged her away and led her to bed where she lay in a stupour.

But life had to go on. Grief had to be contained for the sake of Elizabeth's children and Louis' other relatives. Gradually Elizabeth regained her equilibrium but she was now in changed circumstances. She had been the wife of the ruler, now she was merely a foreign princess in a court far from her own land. Once she had been revered as a charitable woman, her excesses in this area being overlooked because of the position held by her husband who had defended her lavish almsgiving. Now she was accused of wasting revenues that should have been part of her son's patrimony. Elizabeth faced a loneliness that was compounded of many factors which all combined to crush her when she was at her most vulnerable

The story that Elizabeth was forced to leave the Wartburg in the midst of winter does not seem born out by the facts. She went of her own free will.

The confusion that surrounded the aftermath of Louis' death and the way in which Elizabeth had become marginalised at court led to her not receiving the money that was due to her as part of her dower. Deprived of this, she was without the means to procure food that would ensure that she kept to Conrad's directives. True to her conscience she deliberately chose poverty and hardship over an ease that, to her, would compromise her integrity. 'She did not want to receive her food by theft or by exploitation of the poor . . . instead she chose to be humbled and to earn her bread like a hireling by the labour of her own hands.' The words are Guda's as she testified to her mistress' plight.

It seems that the final step was precipitated by some unknown happening and in the event Elizabeth left the Wartburg without proper preparations made for her lodging. She, Guda and Ysentrude made their way down from the castle to the town of Eisenach and there Elizabeth and her companions spent the night in an abandoned pigstye.

Rising early in the morning Elizabeth approached the Franciscans who were gathering for the Office of Matins and asked them to sing the *Te Deum* on her behalf. Poverty and contempt were her portion and she wanted to show that she accepted her lot gladly.

One is irresitably reminded of St. Francis' desription of perfect joy as related in the following story from the *Fioretti*. Francis and Brother Leo were on their way to St. Mary of the Angels, the friars' chief gathering place where the Order was founded. It was wintertime and Francis turned to Brother Leo and said: 'If the friars had the gift of preaching so as to convert whole worlds, if they could drive out devils and heal all kinds of sickness, if they had the gift of prophecy and all knowledge, note carefully that this would not be perfect joy.' Enquiring of Francis in what *did* perfect joy consist, Brother Leo received this answer: 'If, when we arrive at St. Mary of the Angels all covered with mud and exhausted with hunger, drenched with rain and trembling from the cold, and when we knock the porter comes angrily to answer and refuses to let us in, saying we are not friars but imposters sponging on the generosity of good people. And if he beats us with sticks and kicks us back out into the mud and snow. And if we bear all these injuries with patience and joy in union with the sufferings of our Blessed Lord, write down this, Brother Leo, that *here* is perfect joy'.

Elizabeth, like Francis, was being invited to taste of 'perfect joy' in a way that she could never have foreseen. The next day she sent for her children to join her and Guda went to the castle to fetch them: Hermann, a delicate lad of five, Sophia, a strong-willed little girl of nearly three and the infant Gertrude. Elizabeth was confident that someone in the town would offer hospitality but she was mistaken. Word had already got about that she was out of favour with Henry Raspe the new regent. Despite the fact that she had been the support of so many when she had money and rank behind her, no one dared risk the wrath of Henry by sheltering his disgraced sister-in-law. She and her family had to fend for themselves as best they could among the very poor.

An incident from this time relates how one day, when Elizabeth was on her way to church, she encountered an old woman who had previously been a recipient of Elizabeth's bounty, even being personally nursed by her during an illness, It had been raining and the road was a morass of mud and gravel except for a few stepping stones which enabled folk to walk free of the wet. Elizabeth had already set out on the stones when the woman, coming from the other direction, continued to approach in such a way that one or other must step into the mud. Instead of pitying the state of the former

Landgravine it was obvious that this woman now gloried in seeing her humiliated. She roughly pushed Elizabeth out of the way and caused her to fall, soiling her garments. It seemed to make no impression on Elizabeth. She got up laughing gaily and set about washing her clothes at the first opportunity. It is the first record of laughter since Louis' death. She made the best of a bad job in this instance and appears to have been genuinely amused at her change of fortune.

Another day, in Lent, having spent a long time in prayer, Elizabeth developed a fever, not surprising considering the strain under which she was forced to live, her uncertainty regarding the future and the physical hardships attendant on poverty. In the midst of her shivering she suddenly fixed her gaze on the window, laughing softly, her face shining with joy, lost in contemplation. After a short while she shed tears, then her face resumed its happy mien.

Ysentrude, who questioned her lovingly, was told by Elizabeth that the Lord Jesus had appeared to her to console her for her many trials; but then he had turned away as if to leave, hence the tears. Turning his face towards her once more he then said: 'If you wish to be with me I will be with you' and Elizabeth had answered in the words Ysentrude had heard spoken aloud: 'So, my Lord, you wish to remain with me and I with you and never do I wish to be separated from you'. A sentence spoken in a state of fever, but an indication of Elizabeth's choice of Christ even in the midst of pain, and her desire never to be parted from the One she loved above all others.

At last Elizabeth was offered asylum by her aunt, her mother's youngest sister who was abbess of Kitzingen in Lower Franconia. Abbess Matilda received her niece kindly and eventually passed her on to her brother Eckbert, the Prince Bishop of Bamburg. Eckbert, unaware of Elizabeth's vow of continence in the event of Louis' death, tried to persuade her to remarry, even using threats to impose his wishes.

The Emperor himself offered his hand, but Elizabeth was not amenable to persuasion. Unlike most royal brides the death of her husband had not brought relief from a loveless marriage; it had been a relationship that would be a sacrilege for her to try and duplicate. Forunately Elizabeth was saved from further embarassment because at this point her uncle sent for her to reverence the bones of Louis just then brought back from Otranto for burial in his own country.

On returning from the Crusades Louis' vassals had disinterred the body, boiling away the flesh until the bones shone white. These were then wrapped in fine silk, placed in caskets and strapped on mules. A jewelled cross rested on top of the remains so that those who passed the cortège would know that a prince had died for his faith. Every night the caskets were brought to a church where they rested until the journey was resumed the following day. By the end of April or the beginning of May the procession reached Bamberg and Elizabeth was brought to view her husband's bones where they rested, in the cathedral which housed the relics of another married couple, St. Henry the Emperor and his wife St. Cunegunda.

After a great concourse of clerics and townsfolk had accompanied her to the cathedral with psalms and laments, the caskets were opened and Elizabeth saw the white bones glistening on the silk. So this was all that was left of the man she had loved with her whole heart! Full of tears she lifted her eyes heavenwards exclaiming: 'Lord, I give you thanks for having mercifully consoled me with these bones of my husband which I have so much desired. Great as was my love for him you know that I do not regret the sacrifice my beloved offered to you for the liberation of the Holy Land. If I could have him back, I would give the whole world in exchange even though I had to beg with him for ever. But I call upon you to witness that, if it were against your will, I would not want to redeem his life even if it cost but a single hair. Now I recommend him and I recommend myself to your grace. Let your will be accomplished in us. '

Note how closely Elizabeth aligns herself with Louis, how she still misses him. But her extreme grief has been transmuted into calm surrender - 'your will be done in us' - though she would rather have had him back that they could be together even as beggars.

In hearing Elizabeth's outpoured thanksgiving at the sight

of the bones no onlooker would be deceived into thinking she could be persuaded into a second marriage, that at least must have given some comfort to those who had brought the bones back for their eventual burial in Rheinhardsbrunn cloister. Louis' knights were dismayed to find their former Landgravine so close to destitution and they ensured that all revenues due to her were restored.

But by this time Elizabeth had fully renounced all the trappings of royalty. If Louis were not alive to share her indigence she would endure it alone and from choice.

It is difficult to follow a chronological outline of Elizabeth's life at this point. She remained under Conrad's direction and continued her nursing, meanwhile earning a living by spinning wool. Her maids, who were her friends, remained with her and joined in her charitable enterprises. But her children were well-born and her son would be Landgrave in due course.

As she had been provided for as a child, so now she provided for her own children. They were a last link with the life she was putting behind her in obedience, as she saw it, to the divine invitation to follow Christ poor, naked, crucified.

Hermann and Sophia went to the castle of Kreuzberg, one of Louis' palaces, where Henry Raspe would initiate Hermann into his duties as a future ruler. Sophia, when she was old enough, was married to the Duke of Brabant. Through her, the British royal family can trace their descent to St. Elizabeth as can most of the former royal families of Europe. Little Gertrude was placed in the Altenburg monastery, a Promonstratensian foundation, as Louis and Elizabeth had already decided. In due course Gertrude herself came to be honoured as a saint though most likely owing to the reflected glory of her mother rather than through any indication of great personal sanctity. The infant was received kindly by the nuns and there is evidence that she continued to visit her mother while Elizabeth still lived.

In choosing poverty Elizabeth finalised her decision by a public act. In the chapel of the Friars Minor at Eisenach with her hands clasped on the altar she had given them, she renounced 'her own will, her earthly estates and all that the saviour commands us in the Gospel to put aside', as Conrad wrote later.

Towards the end of that year Elizabeth followed Conrad to Marburg. It was against his wishes, but she persisted. The town had been given her as part of her dower and she was determined to move far from a world that she had renounced. There, with Guda and Ysentrude, she made her profession in the Franciscan Third Order. The three adopted the grey tunic worn by the *Sisters of Penance*, as the Tertiaries were called.

It was the end of an era for Elizabeth and the dawn of a new way of living that would confirm her in sanctity because of her Christlikeness.

Franciscan Sister

I have been crucified with Christ;
and it is no longer I that live but Christ who lives in ne.
And the life I now live in the flesh
I live by faith in the Son of God, who loved ne and gave himself for me.
Gal. 2:19-20

Elizabeth's affinity with Francis had grown over the years since the Friars came to Thuringia. She had already renounced everything that might be termed earthly riches when she laid her hands on the altar at Eisenach. Now she took the further step of officially receiving the Franciscan habit, the habit of penance and poverty.

There can be no doubt that, with her wealth and high birth, Elizabeth could have entered any monastery she chose and lived there in a way consonant with her royal rank. She would have been an abbess surrounded by servants, and from her safe enclosure she could have distributed alms through subordinates without having to touch a sick or verminous person with her own hands. But Elizabeth crossed the social divide completely. She wanted to *be* poor as much as she wanted to *serve* the poor. She did not want to be a nun addressed as 'my Lady', waited on by others, administering abbatial estates, like the Landgravine she had been while Louis lived. Neither did she aspire to become a Poor Clare, much as the life must have appealed with its stress on personal poverty. It would not have been difficult for Elizabeth to found a monastery of Poor Ladies in Thuringia as her cousin Agnes had done in Prague. But what Elizabeth wanted was poverty with and among the poor, and she lived at the time when this unusual option was mde available for her through the Franciscan Third Order.

From the first, Francis had attracted men who wanted to share his itinerant lifestyle. They worked for a living, preached to the ordinary people, made the reality of Christ live for the masses through inaugurating popular devotions, and were free from the trappings that went with a settled monastic lifestyle. Poverty was their ideal, a poverty that gave them

freedom to move about to wherever they were needed, poverty that clothed them in garments of grey sacking, poverty that enabled them to find joy in what was common to all: the birds, the flowing water, the sun . . . without trying to hold on to and possess things for themselves.

The Poor Ladies, under Clare's leadership, had adopted an enclosed life, living poorly and simply within the confines of their convents. But this was a specialised calling and did not have the universal appeal that the friars were able to exercise with their wider outreach and closeness to those in need.

So another form of life had gradually emerged among those who wanted to share Francis' spirit but could be neither friars nor Clares; either because of family obligations or simply because they did not think themselves called to a more formal religious consecration. After all, if Francis wanted only to follow the Gospel as literally as possible this could not be an option only for an élite. It must be seen as a challenge open to everyone who desired intimacy with Christ in poverty, penance, simplicity and joy.

The informal lay following of the Franciscan path penetrated all classes of society and found expression in any number of ways. There were hermits, penitents, married men and women, secular priests. . . . . some tertiaries even banded together to form communities dedicated explicitly to charitable work and lived as religious with a common habit and timetable. All were involved in spreading the message of the Poverello to others.

For these followers Francis wrote a *Letter to all the Faithful* exhorting all to a life of penance and charity. This letter now exists in three versions, but the first two show Francis' original spirit more clearly as also his personal interest in the Third Order. He writes:

> How happy and blest are those who love the Lord and do as the Lord himelf commands in the Gospel: 'You shall love the Lord your God with all your heart and with all your soul, and your neighbour as yourself'. Let us therefore bear fruits that befit repentance. And let us love our neighbours as ourselves. Let us have charity and humility and let us give alms, for this cleanses the soul of the stains of sin . . . We should not be

wise and prudent according to worldly standards, but rather we should be simple, humble and pure. We should never desire to be above others but rather we should be servants and subject for the Lord's sake to every human authority. Upon all who do these things and endure to the end will rest the spirit of the Lord. He will make his dwelling place and home in them and they will be children of their heavenly Father whose works they do; and they are spouses and brothers and mothers of our Lord Jesus Christ.

A later version of the Letter reveals the influence of Francis' friend and legislator, Cardinal Hugolino, who had earlier compiled a Rule for the *Humiliati*, a lay movement based in Lombardy. This other document is more practical in its directives, taking into account the different experiences of those who were living according to Franciscan principles and stressing the Catholic nature of their faith and commitment.

In the final version there is almost a purely legislative tone which has lost the earlier spontaneity and vision, but which was to stand the Third Order in good stead for many years. Like all legislative documents it is dry. It needs to be read and interpreted within the whole ambience of Franciscan tradition and lived experience.

In this Rule the Brothers and Sisters are bound to a severe simplicity of dress. Even the price and texture of the garments is fixed so that all appearance of luxury is outlawed. They are bound to fasting and abstinence on certain days, are to eschew banquets and stage plays, are forbidden to bear arms. They are to live at peace with their neighbours, practise works of charity and receive the Sacraments three times a year. Like the religious Orders proper they are to recite the hours of the breviary. Those who cannot read are to say a corresponding number of Our Fathers.

The whole concept of the Third Order challenges the pomp and worldliness of feudal society but its chief glory lies in the spirit of loving compassion and simple devotion that inspired the early penitents. It made them friends of the lepers and outcasts as well as supporting them in becoming men and women of prayer.

Sometimes the brothers and sisters of an area would form

basic communities to help the sick and poor, living a common life and wearing a form of religious habit. This had the advantage of conferring a definite status on their work. They were forerunners of more modern apostolic congregations, many of whom still look to these early groups as their founding inspiration. They were also able to meet specific local needs whether it was nursing, catechising, or promoting honesty in trade or commerce.

Poverty continued to be for the Third Order the *leitmotiv* it had been for the early friars and Poor Clares. Angela of Foligno, a penitent of the second generation of Franciscans who was acclaimed as one who rekindled the fire of the Franciscan spirit when the friars themselves had grown cold, proclaimed the preeminence of poverty in words such as these:

> Pride can only exist in those who possess anything or believe that they possess anything.
> Humility exists only in those who are so poor that they have nothing, for poverty is an exceedingly great good. Poverty is the root and mother of all humility and all good. For whoever has poverty can never come to ruin or fall into deception.
> This is the highest and continual and most perfect poverty of the God-Man Jesus Christ, Saviour of all who although he was the Lord of riches, yet chose to be poor among us, that he might inspire us to love poverty also.
>
> For he was poor indeed, in will and in spirit, more than any creature can fathom for the sake of the infinite and most sweet love with which he loved us.
> Poor I say and needy as a beggar.
> Poor in temporal things,
> poor in friends,
> poor in power,
> poor in worldly wisdom,
> poor in fame of sanctity,
> poor in state of dignity,
> poor in all things.
>
> He preached poverty and declared the poor were blessed and

that one day they would be the judges of the world. [1]

Poverty and the love of Christ were intertwined for the Franciscan; poverty and the service of the poor, poverty and the freedom to respond to need, poverty and prayer, poverty and simplicity of life. For Elizabeth this was a far cry from the religious life lived by others of her class who chose the cloister.

While at the Wartburg she had built a hospital and nursed the inmates even while still married to Louis. But the life she now elected to share with her faithful maids was the life of the genuinely poor combined with the service of the poor. She dressed humbly and washed dishes as a servant, not a mistress of servants.

Elizabeth continued to have Conrad as her director, indeed it was for this reason she had followed him to Marburg; but she was afraid of him and his harshness. It makes us cringe to see the contrast in her relationship with this man and with Louis. With Louis the relationship had been one of autonomy and mutuality, with Conrad it was one of power and subservience. However it seems that Elizabeth did contrive to keep as much of her freedom as was possible in the circumstances. For instance, Conrad forbade her to give away more than a penny at a time. She mischievously circumvented this by giving only one penny as directed but allowing recipients to rejoin the queue immediately and come for another . . . . and answer . . . Conrad's was a restraining influence on a woman who would otherwise have gone to any extreme of poverty and service to compensate for the years when she had known plenty.

Conrad ultimately tested Elizabeth to the point of sending away Guda and Ysentrude and replacing them with people of his own choosing. These made life difficult for the former Landgravine and reported on her to Conrad thus sowing an atmosphere of distrust. One was a laybrother who attended to her affairs, one a girl of lowly birth, and the last a noblewoman deaf and extremely severe. For most of the time Elizabeth continued to earn her living by spinning wool for the Altenburg monastery.

---

[1] From Chs. 55 & 59 of *The Visions and Instructions of Blessed Angela of Foligno* by Bro. Arnold OFM. Trans. by a secular priest. Richardson, 1871

The King of Hungary, hearing from some travellers of the manner of life his daughter had embraced, sent word that she would be welcome to return to her homeland. She briskly repulsed the envoys and their retinue. She had chosen Louis and his people as her own. To return to the country of her birth would be to abandon the people she had grown to love and whom she now served in her poverty.

Elizabeth's love for poverty extended even to the ornamentation of churches, where rich display was taken as a sign of piety. One day, when visiting a monastery where the religious had a sumptuously decorated church but relied on charitable donations for their daily sustenance she said: 'It were better for the money to be spent on food and clothing, rather than for decorating the walls, for you should bear these images in your hearts.' A veiled rebuke that religious should not live surrounded by the trappings of wealth even if only in their churches. To beg, while having the means to purchase luxuries, was equivalent to stealing what belonged to the really poor. For Elizabeth, this sort of thing brought religion into disrepute.

Elizabeth, with part of her dower money, built a hospital just outside the walls of Marburg where the sick could be nursed by her and other Franciscan Tertiaries. She had the hospital dedicated to St. Francis who had been canonised the previous year, 1227. For her own dwelling Elizabeth built herself a hut in the centre of the hospital courtyard where she could be continually available for whatever services were needed.

Many stories are told of this period of Elizabeth's life, detailing her attentions to those who suffered from repulsive diseases, especially the tenderness she showered on children who were the most vulnerable and pathetic victims. She would take them to eat at her table, washing their soiled linen and rising during the night to see that their needs of nature were attended to.

Elizabeth took literally the words of Christ: 'Whatever you do to the least of these you do to me'. She really saw him present in the sick and found them a route to his humanity, ever present in those who needed her care. Hence the joy with which she cleansed sores and dressed wounds. To her the sick were Jesus himself living upon earth in the humblest and poorest of his creatures, and so each one was precious, giving a glimpse into the window of eternity,

Five hundred marks were still left to Elizabeth after the hospital was built and endowed. She decided to distribute this money herself in a novel way that has been described by one who was present on the occasion. For twelve miles around Elizabeth had the poor informed that they should gather in a certain place on an appointed day. When they were assembled she had them sit down while she passed among them serving them and washing their feet. A whole cross section of humanity was there; children, the very old, the sick, the poverty stricken the miserable and homeless. . . Elizabeth moved along the lines smiling, full of joy that she could give the last of her wealth to those who needed it most.

In this case all were forbidden to leave their places until everyone had received alms. But one young woman did not hear the decree; she moved among the seated people looking for her crippled sister who had come for the royal bounty. All unaware of her fault, the girl was brought before Elizabeth for disobedience, the punishment of which was the cutting off of a lock of hair.

Now the girl, Hildegunde, had a mass of beautiful dark curls. Elizabeth, suddenly inspired, ordered all her hair to be cut off. Poor Hildegunde began to sob uncontrollably, trying to explain the mistake. Elizabeth was adamant. The hair was shorn and then Elizabeth asked her kindly if she had ever thought of embracing a better form of life! The girl confessed that for a long time she had thought of becoming a religious but her beautiful hair had stood in the way: she could not bear to let it go. Now it was gone anyway and so she decided to cast in her lot with Elizabeth. At the time she told of this incident Hildegunde was still at the Marburg hospital nursing the sick as a Franciscan sister.

Night came and the moon rose above the gathering. The money was all distributed. Many of the poor had left but there was still a goodly number of sick and crippled who had decided to stay within the hospital enclosure for the night rather than set out on the long journey home. Elizabeth, who had retired, saw them still sitting in the courtyard. 'Since the weaker ones have stayed let us give them something more,' she proposed. She gave each a portion of bread and some small coins so that they should not spend the night hungry. Then she had fires lit to warm them, and she moved among them once more, soothing their limbs and stroking their lice-infected heads.

The poor, deeply touched by this love so humbly expressed, began to sing. The smiling Elizabeth beneath the moon, the baskets of bread, the song rising into the night from hundreds of throats gathered around the flickering fires, present a picture that expresses something of the heart of Elizabeth of Hungary. Not only did she relieve need, but she delighted in seeing others happy and in doing all she could to make them so. Elizabeth is a thoroughly human saint. She had known separation from loved ones, physical bereavement, sickness, alienation, cold and disappointment. But she did not exhort others to bear suffering stoically. She wanted always to inject a note of joy into human lives, however impoverished.

In the rest of the time left to her Elizabeth was often seen not only in the hospital, but distributing alms and food, clothing and bedding in the hovels and lazar houses of the vicinity. For this she sold the remainder of her valuables, her jewels, rings, dresses. She had no more use for these tokens. Let everything be given to the poor to whom it rightly belonged anyway.

Holiness acknowledged

Even though our outer nature is wasting away, our inner nature is being renewed day by day. For this slight weight of affliction is preparing for us an eternal weight of glory beyond all measure. Because we look not at what can be seen but at what cannot be seen; for what can be seen is temporary but what cannot be seen is eternal.
2 Cor. 4: 16-18

Elizabeth was now at the apex of the spiritual life. She had given herself completely to Christ and his poor, kept back nothing for herself. It was three years since Louis had died and she was bereft of husband and children. It would be a comfort if we knew that now she had attained peace and happiness in her chosen way of life, but it was not as simple as that.

Conrad remained a shadow on her horizon. He had imposed on her penances and detachments that she had never foreseen, such as the order to dismiss her faithful companions Guda and Ysentrude and live with disagreeable servants. He had ruled on her almsgiving and curtailed her nursing of some of the worst cases. But that he backed his injunctions with harsh physical punishments for the slightest infringement of his commands reveals a streak of sadism that one finds extremely hard to come to terms with.

That Elizabeth saw Conrad as an instrument used by God for her sanctification did not lessen her fear of him and of his reactions which were often arbitrary and inhuman. One time he severely birched her bare back for entering an enclosure of nuns. He had given permission for this but did not expect her to take advantage of it. Elizabeth bore the marks of the lash for more than three weeks and her friends, who were included in the punishment, did not find it easy to forgive such a hard master. Today we have a very different attitude towards physical violence but at least this and similar incidents show that Elizabeth did not only experience joy in giving: that would would be only natural and understandable. She also knew the struggle for self-conquest as she strove to submit to injustice meekly, as indeed the poor have to do many times in their existence.

There is generosity here, a hint of the supreme sacrifice hidden under a smile. It was the smile of a widow whose love for her deceased husband remained undinted, yet not a word of sorrow or complaint had passed her lips since the outburst at Bamberg. Now she knew she had to forget self in order to think of others. She had to hide her own grief and loneliness-indeed she had to love it because it gave her privileged access to the Christ she loved supremely.

Suffering, interior and exterior, was nevertheless taking its toll on her body and Elizabeth surmised that death was near. She was twenty-four when she fell sick. There is no diagnosis available as to what proved to be a fatal illness but Elizabeth knew her hours were numbered and that life for her had run its course. The thread of her life, wound round the golden ball of love, was winding its last round before it entered the gates of the heavenly Jerusalem. The nobles of Thuringia, who only recently had treated her as a mad woman, now realised the treasure they were losing. They came frequently to her poor room until she asked that all secular persons be dismissed, with the exception of a poor boy whom she had adopted and nursed back to health from a pitiable condition.

Conrad came to hear her confession and to receive her directives as to what was to happen to her few poor belongings. Everything was to be given to the poor except for the patched grey tunic she wore and in which she wanted to be buried.

After Conrad had departed it seemed to Elizabeth that she heard sweet singing, in which she joined with her tuneful treble, as if death held no fears for her. It was night when the end came, but for her the Day without ending was just beginning.

* * *

Elizabeth is something of an enigma even now. She has left no doctrine, no writings, no spiritual 'way' that she exhorts others to emulate. She was born to a life in royal society and yet she was always totally natural and unconventional in her behaviour. She was never quite what was expected of her station either in girlhood, marriage or the religious life she eventually embarked on. She is surprising at every turn yet unexpectedly 'all of a piece'. In Elizabeth we see a woman of integrity bent upon living her Christian life to the full in whatever circumstances she found herself.

Love is the lodestar of most women's lives and Elizabeth was consistent only in her determination to respond to love, human and divine, in whatever way she could. This quest led her to experience the rapture of a pure physical and sexual relationship with the man she loved, just as it led her to the depths of poverty and deprivation on her husband's death. The golden thread of love runs through her life stretched to the uttermost in self-giving to others and an all-pervading devotion to Christ, poor and crucified. It culminated in the desire to be totally conformed to Christ's likeness in humility and total abandonment. Significantly, Elizabeth is one of the few medieval women saints commemorated in the calender of the universal Church. Contemporaries such as Mechtilde, Gertrude the Great, Hedwig of Silesia, are optional memorials or assigned only to a particular order or country. But Elizabeth has retained her universal appeal. Despite her designation as Elizabeth of Hungary she is revered above all in her adopted homeland. She is the great inspiration of the Germanic peoples as well as the patroness of numerous communities of women dedicated to the works of mercy.

Elizabeth's place in the Franciscan Third Order is one of preeminence. Together with St. Louis of France she is its principal patron, and her picture is in evidence in the great basilica of St. Francis in Assisi. There she is seen dressed in royal robes and looking in profile every inch a woman who knew how to make her mark in society. But a later Gobelin vestment, also in Assisi, which depicts the tree of the Franciscan Order, portrays her more truly. There, Francis is embroidered in the centre and from him branch out the great Saints whom he inspired and who followed his Rule, popes and cardinals among that number. Two women figure in the design, both close to Francis: Clare, foundress of the Poor Clares, and Elizabeth. Clare is garbed as a nun holding the Blessed Sacrament in a monstrance. This recalls the incident when, bearing the Sacrament aloft she repelled invaders who were threatening the city and convent. Elizabeth, on the other hand, is in the plainest of dresses girded with a knotted cord, much plainer than Clare. Her veil is white, for only a professed nun is entitled to the double veil of black on white. Elizabeth holds in her hands the symbols of her dedication. In her left is the crown she laid aside when she chose poverty; in her right is the cloak St. Francis is said to have sent her as a mark of gratitude for establishing the Order in Germany. But she holds both crown and cloak away from her body. She clings to nothing, not even the holiest memento. Elizabeth had wanted Christ alone and in the end that desire was fulfilled. The rest to her was abolutely nothing.

* * *

The affection of Elizabeth's own people is evident in the cathedral that arose in Marburg soon after her death and whose foundation stone was laid by her brother-in-law, Conrad, who had become Grand Master of the Teutonic Knights, a military Order in the Crusader tradition. He poured the wealth of his Order into a memorial he considered fitting for the recently despised Landgravine, widow of his own brother and now acclaimed as a holy woman.

Marburg Cathedral has been called the greatest monument to a woman other than Our Lady. There Elizabeth was entombed, her remains being brought from Marburg hospital chapel with great ceremonial. For this solemn transfer not only the notables of Hungary and Thuringia, France and Bohemia were present, but almost the entire family of Elizabeth, including the dowager duchess Sophia, widow of Hermann I, Elizabeth's mother-in-law, who had left the Cistercian convent where she lived in retirement so as to be present at the ceremony. Then there was Henry Raspe, who had been instrumental in his sister-in-law's expulsion from the Wartburg after Louis' death. With him was Hermann II, Elizabeth's son and the reigning Landgrave (who would die at the age of eighteen with no descendants), and her two daughters: Sophia, an elegant twelve year old princess, and Gertrude, nine, brought from the monastery of Altenburg. Pilgrims who had been coming to beg Elizabeth's intercession since her death were there also, marvelling at the sweet oil that seemed to flow from the bones of the saint. The Emperor himself witnessed the transfer of the body that May 1st, 1263. It was a strange coincidence that this very emperor had once hoped to marry the woman he now came to venerate as a canonised saint.

Everything had come full circle.

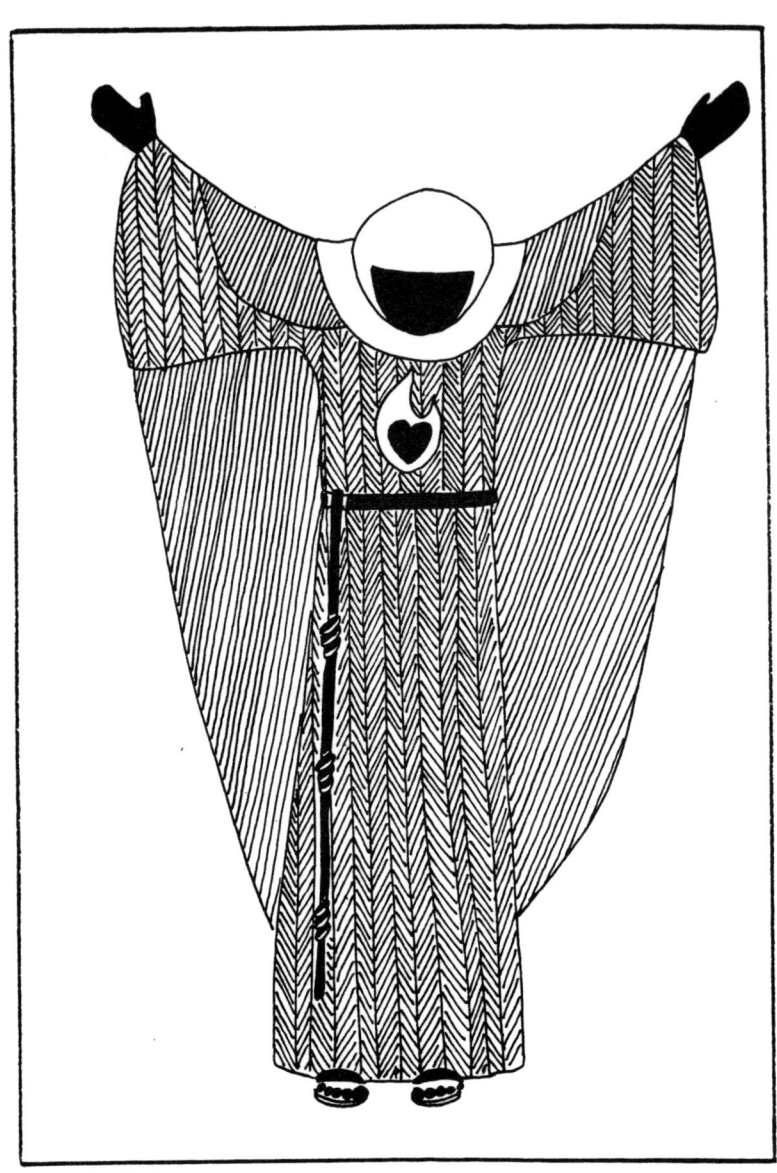

Only love remains

If I speak in the tongues of mortals and angels but do not have love, I am a noisy gong or a clanging cymbal. And if I have prophetic powers, and understand all mysteries and all knowledge, and if I have faith so as to remove mountains, but do not have love, I am nothing.
If I give away all my possessions and if I hand over my body so that I may boast, but do not have love, I gain nothing.
Love is patient, love is kind; love is not envious or boastful or arrogant or rude. It does not insist on its own way; it is not irritable or resentful; it does not rejoice in wrongdoing but rejoices in the truth. It bears all things, believes all things, hopes all things, endures all things.
ICor. 13: 1-17

Love has always been considered the key to the spiritual life, love of God and love of others. Yet many saints seem to have stifled natural love in favour of the divine, and in so doing to have bent their own natures out of shape. In very few are human love and love of God in such harmony that the personality is enhanced by both.

In Elizabeth this harmony occurred to an extraordinary degree as we have seen; not without struggle, for naturalness is not formlessness. Elizabeth did not let her natural urges run wild or unpruned. With a strong resolve she resolved to love Christ to her utmost limits; to love with the very love of Christ so as ultimately to be conformed to him as the Crucified One.

The gift of loving is a gift, an exceptional gift that carries within it the perils associated with any exceptional endowment. Love can sweep one away on a tide of uncontrollable passion, but the person so swept is often nearer to being a saint than the exemplary citizen who knows nothing of such powerful forces. The most human feature of Elizabeth was that she was gifted with a heart hiding forces of love that few tap. Her natural life and her sanctity sprang from the same root, an immense capacity for self donation and the determination to love at whatever cost.

Elizabeth's was an active love, one that went out to others in a thousand practical ways. She was not the contemplative 'type', the retiring, prayerful, nun-like woman. Rather she was a woman overflowing with active love, the love that most of us have to practise in the wider world. It was the love of a St. Francis, nourished by prayer, leading to prayer, but having to find an outlet as Francis found it: serving the lepers, nursing the poor, binding up sores both physical and spiritual. It was a love that found its first expression within the ambience of family and friends, and from there spread out to an ever widening circle. Elizabeth had wealth, yet even in using this she chose to give until it hurt, give beyond the bounds of propriety, just as she gave of her love, freely and selflessly.

Elizabeth, nourished and sustained by love, grew to understand love's costliness and the detachment necessary for love to reach maturity. Her heart had literally to be stretched to breaking point: for God and for others.

John of the Cross divides the serious spiritual journey into two stages, the active and passive nights. The active night consists in what *we* do to further our union with God; the passive is what *God* does. John speaks of beginners in the ways of God, who resolutely give of themselves and their possessions and do so generously, according to their perception of God's demands. But sanctity is not something we can attain by our own efforts, however generous and well intentioned. It is the work of God alone. It is a work that the soul must cooperate with, submitting the will to all that God asks in the way of prayer and sacrifice.

Elizabeth had begun to live a serious spiritual life from an early age. We have only to recall her attraction to prayer, her childish efforts at self denial in playing games, her little ruses to visit the chapel frequently without attracting too much comment.

It would be good here to look at the active night in Elizabeth's life in case we should conclude, mistakenly, that life was all easy and sweet for her as she progressed in age and wisdom. Like everyone else, Elizabeth had to make sustained efforts to purify and direct her affections. She had to work in such a way that her actions and charitable enterprises were directed into the channels that would eventually immerse her in the sea of God's love, more boundless than any ocean. She could not have sustained the purification of God's hand in the passive night that later engulfed her, had she not first cooperated to the best of her ability with the first impulses of grace.

Elizabeth's earnestness in giving herself to God was first expressed through her attraction to poverty and the poor. She had wealth and could keep it, spend it or give it away. She chose the path of giving. This was the exterior manifestation of a growing interior disposition.

And so Elizabeth gave of her riches. She gave from her abundance in the form of money, food and clothing, but she extended her giving onto another level: the level of her time, her service, her care, her personal involvement. In other words, through exterior things she gave of her inner self in a way that was costly. This fidelity to the dictates of her heart and her conscience fostered a personal integrity rare for a woman of her station. How could it be considered improper to take gifts to the poor herself, to speak to them in a friendly manner as an equal and not as a superior? After all, did not everyone share a common humanity? Why should she not go into their hovels and nurse them in their fevers and plagues? Elizabeth did not choose to be stubborn and disobedient, rather she chose to listen to the voice of Christ in the Gospel proclaiming that what we do to others we do to him. Therefore, in the long run, Elizabeth was unable to live among the conventional who are guided in their actions by institutional mores and age old habits of thought. In such a universe each person has his or her place and the classes do not meet and intermingle as brothers and sisters in Christ. They are fixed within a hierarchy where there can be no mutuality, no partnership, only inferiors and superiors.

It was identification with the poor that enabled Elizabeth to accept the strict dietary laws imposed on her by Conrad of Marburg and to go hungry at the royal table. This silent witness caused those about her to question their own conduct in justice towards the needy. Even when abstention must have implied a criticism of her beloved husband, Elizabeth's resolve did not waver.

As Elizabeth struggled to give God the first place in her heart she must have felt the costliness of it. It was only natural to abandon herself to the love she felt for Louis. She could have idolised her husband, lost her own personality in the desire to please him, let her role as loving wife and mother become her life's work while stifling her other obligations under the plea that now she must think only of her partner. Yet she made the *gesture* of detachment when she rose during the night to pray while still clasping Louis' hand. She could not manage the fullness of the gift, yet she did what she could in the gesture. It was the symbol that God was her first love.

However, there was an untramelled streak in Elizabeth's behaviour when it came to what conventional piety required of a wife and mother. She had no fear of the flesh in itself. She did not try to 'edify' her entourage by suppressing her passion. She was openly filled with desire for Louis' caresses. She felt the anguish of being separated from him when he was absent. It was because her love was so ardent, so consuming, that she realised that its very beauty and preciousness might become an obstacle, not because it was a wrong love, but because it was a reflection of the even greater love of God that possessed her as she matured.

But whatever tensions there were in Elizabeth's marital relationship as she melded together the human and divine elements of her love, the sensual with the spiritual, she had always envisaged her future as being with Louis no matter what else transpired. At his death she was doubly bereft: of his physical presence and of his understanding support. This was the end of her own choices. It was now for *God* to choose and show his will through a new set of circumstances.

Elizabeth was therefore ready for the passive night as it was worked out in her own life: not through darkness in contemplative prayer but through the darkness of bereavement and loneliness, misunderstanding and pain.

There are some who would see the last period of Elizabeth's life as a contradiction of what had gone before; the gracious and spontaneous princess assumes the form of a grim ascetic. But in reality her life did not change direction, nor did she become a different person. She was the same Elizabeth facing a new phase of life and putting upon it the stamp of her love expressed through a different medium. St. Francis, whose spirituality ever beckoned her to further horizons, promises freedom from all that would hold or enslave the person, and this freedom has to be found in *all* circumstances. When trials come they must not hamper but liberate the one who suffers, for one must find in these very trials the means of coming closer to God. We are to find God within the circumstances of life, not outside them. All can be affirmed, all can be turned to joy, because there is nothing outside the ambience of God who permeates and penetrates the whole of creation.

Elizabeth was subjected to the demands of a harsh confessor, to exile and alienation, to the loss of her children and lifelong companions. These were the means by which she obscurely intuited God's hand completing the work he had begun, breaking the vessel of her *persona* so that the inner form could emerge: the final form of the crucified Son of God, living once more in her flesh as he had lived in Francis' through the impression of the stigmata. Elizabeth's body bore no exterior stigmata save the stretch marks of child birth, the calloused hand of worker and nurse. But these were every bit as holy and Christlike as the wounds of Francis. They were the wounds of life itself.

The true following of Christ in nakedness and poverty does not consist in being a beautiful and fulfilled person but in allowing God to mould us into the image of his crucified Son. Only in this is real fulfilment and Elizabeth knew it even if she was not able to articulate her insights and experience in theological language.

She was one of those practical persons whose way of living speaks for them, whose fruits show the beauty of the plant and the depth of its roots even while they busy themselves with tasks that seem commonplace. Such are the lives of thousands of people who alleviate the suffering of others while not averting to their own, whose lives are a tissue of human love and human bereavement, of service to the sick, of familial relationships, of prayer in darkness and of blind clinging to the will of God as it unfolds day by day. Such persons are without pretensions, and to speak to them of the nights of St. John of the Cross would evoke a brisk shake of the head and a denial that they are following the path of contemplation. But they are – and in the very obscurity and darkness John refers to.

Love purified

As God's chosen ones, holy and beloved, clothe yourselves with compassion, kindness, humility, meekness and patience. Bear with one another and, if anyone has a complaint against another, forgive each other; just as the Lord has forgiven you, so you also must forgive. Above all, clothe yourselves in love, which binds everything together in perfect harmony.
Col. 3: 12-14.

We can consider Elizabeth's ascent towards sanctity under three aspects of purification: the purification of her love for God, of her love for her neighbour, and in her apostolic vocation.

Outwardly Elizabeth was blessed with many good things: she had wealth, beauty, friends, a loving husband. She had the means to do good and she used them to the full. Then there were her inward qualities: freedom from slavery to convention, piety, high spirits. She was spontaneous in her actions, her emotions were close to the surface and easily expressed.

In her life there was no permature detachment. God had to work in her as she developed, but first she was called to respond on the ordinary human level. As John of the Cross writes to a spiritual seeker:

> Whoever desires nothing but God does not walk in darkness however blind and poor they may feel . . . In what do you imagine the service of God to consist except in abstaining from evil, keeping his commandments and doing his work as well as we can? When you do this, what need have you to seek here and there for other instructions, other lights, other consolations in which there can lurk many snares.
> *Letter* 14

Elizabeth's piety was rooted in the commandments, the Sacraments, the Gospel; in other words, the way of the 'ordinary' Christian, not a member of a religious Order who must assume a certain outward demeanour, a 'spirituality' that interprets the faith in a certain perspective. It was because Elizabeth had the time to grow humanly that she had the necessary foundations laid for her future sanctity. As Ida Gorres writes perceptively:

> Misconceptions of sainthood! They would supply material for a book, not merely for an evening's conversation. But as a beginning I would just say this; that we, today, with all our refined spirituality and our scientific study of religion, our accumulated experience of innumerable Christian generations, our intensive ethical culture, our superior psychological and spiritual methods, our retreats and systematic meditation and all the rest of it; that we, with all this machinery at our disposal and such a mass of good will should see so few really great convincing Christians among us (of course we can't pass any final judgment, but we are told to know them by their fruits) is I venture to say, due to one simple but sufficient cause, we are not human enough to be saints. No, right from the outset, from an utterly false notion of piety, we dare not let ourselves become human beings. A human being is made, not born. We don't let our children grow up into real healthy men and women, we wish them to be simply and solely Christian — and we forget that grace needs a deep, reliable, healthy natural ground if it is to take root and bear a hundredfold; that otherwise the 'supernatural' remains in the air, is unnatural, a phantom without strength of life blood, and will therefore disappear before the first onslaught of real passion, springing from strong, natural roots. We talk of spiritualising and don't even grasp that the word itself implies that there must be something there to spiritualise. [1]

It was because Elizabeth was so humanly unspoiled, so humanly rooted, that her sanctity sprang from the soil of her being and was not a hothouse plant nurtured in an environment screened from the elements. She was hardy not delicate. It was because her nature was so strongly and spontaneously loving that she was led through nature and grace to the 'strong meat' that enabled her to taste of the Cross and find it sustaining.

All the saints have a spiritual attraction that unifies and gives shape to their inner development. Elizabeth's love for the

---

[1] p. 17 Ida Gorres (Coudenhove) *The Nature of Sanctity* Sheed & Ward 1932.

poor, naked, crucified Christ was brought to fruition because she *wanted* this union, not just in pious thought or imagination, but in very truth. God gave her what she really wanted and she was enabled through grace to pay the price.

The soul is given all it desires, says John of the Cross. Most of us desire too little rather than too much. Elizabeth desired *everything*. She had said she wanted poverty and God took her at her word. But this poverty, despite painful deprivation and emotional isolation was a joy that engendered in her a deep peace. Like St. Francis, the most opposite powers were reconciled in her. Joy made them both the most independent and yet the most submissive of all people, in whom a disciplined calm co-existed with demonstrations of deep feeling. Both were able to combine an active will with complete abandonment to the will of God. Theirs was an uncontrived simplicity coupled with downright daring in the supernatural order. Gradually Elizabeth gave up her friends, her children, her accustomed manner of life, her free use of money for charity, her affections and personal desires. In her we can see clearly the path each of us must follow if we are serious in embracing the poverty of the Cross. What must be surrendered is different for each; it is the *disposition* to give that must be identical whether the vocation is contemplative prayer or active love.

We shy away from sacrifice whereas Elizabeth welcomed it with open arms. She knew well that what she was asked to sacrifice was precious, not worthless. In that lay its value. It is not that God wants pain and self denial in themselves, nor did Elizabeth view them in this way. She wanted to give without thought of self, solely to please the One she loved.

A gift given is transparent to a double meaning. It is precious in itself and it stands for the person who gives it as a symbol of the totality of the self. Into all that she gave Elizabeth put the love of her whole heart, begging God to accept what it symbolised: her very person, whole and entire.

Maybe in some of her giving Elizabeth was mistaken. No matter. She too was a fallible human being whose discernment could be imperfect. She had her faults, her weaknesses, and of these she was no doubt more aware than the chroniclers who marvelled at her self-abasement.

Elizabeth was not concerned with making a good impression. She was on the alert to please the Beloved in whatever guise he was present: in her husband, in the poor, in the periods she dedicated to prayer. At each moment she was aware that a gift could be offered to God, an invitation responded to or ignored. She held a precious moment but she held *on* to nothing. At every turn she opened her hands, retaining nothing for self, letting the precious oil of her life be poured out over the feet of Christ and his people.

Elizabeth's dedication to the poor, the sick, the abandoned was, because of her motivating spirit, very different from the well meaning almsgiving that is aroused by mere pity. It was a direct complement of her love for God, a way into meeting Christ, present in each one. It was because Elizabeth loved Jesus that each person revealed a different aspect of him. Even when she was treated with ungratefulness or rudeness she never withdrew her service and her love. She did not give only to the grateful and deserving but to all, for gradually she came to see with the eyes of God himself, the eyes that are all tender, all compassionate. She knew only the privilege of being allowed to give without working out whether or not the recipient was worthy. Her passionate dedication to the sick, her kissing of their sores, was part of her passionate devotion to a Jesus who welcomes sinners, who allows himself to be 'eaten up' by the needy and the crippled, the insane and the diseased, without even having time for a meal, so great was the press of the crowds. That God would accept her service to his children was Elizabeth's privilege, not something regrettable because it took her away from the quiet of interior prayer or even the embrace of her husband.

Real love for others is always purifying. One way that Elizabeth tried to ensure that hers was in accord with the will of God was through obedience to Master Conrad. Thus she did not merely follow her natural bent but allowed it to be channelled by another who kept her humble, even humiliated.

Elizabeth's vocation was truly apostolic in that she permitted herself to be 'sent' in later life, rather than choosing for herself. She stripped herself of everything, even her own will. While despising nothing, she renounced her possessions in order to pass beyond the fragile things of time and partake of eternity.

This was encompassed in a life of intense activity, for true poverty demands both work and service. In Elizabeth action and contemplation were not opposed to one another. At the highest point of her soul they were aspects of the one love which unified her life in Christ and his members: the whole body of the mystical Lord. As Lavelle writes:

> To measure our action we must not be too preoccupied with its success or failure, for this would be to imitate those who refrain from sowing lest the birds devour the grain. The supreme worth of action lies in its being an imitation of God who is himself Pure Act and a participation of his will and of his essence; for the very powers that dispose us to act are given to us by God. By our action we respond to his call, continuing with our own hands and without respite the work of creation itself. The holiness taught by St. Francis is not only, as some suppose, meek, resigned, and attentive. It is also resolute, prompt, eager, enterprising, indefatigable. [1]

Elizabeth's charity did not idealise those she served. She was not blind to their faults, to their human mediocrity, degradation, vicious propensities. She loved with a love based on reality, without 'romantic' overtones. Indeed if one starts to serve others, as many do, with an idealism divorced from facts, one is soon disabused. Daily contact with dirt, pus, wounds hunger, indigence, speedily demands an unromantic and pragmatic response.

Living in a Christian society, Elizabeth exercised her apostolate also in encouraging the sick to use their pain to turn Godward. She wanted those she nursed to go to confession and Communion, to prepare well for death. She did not want to be the focus of their attention; rather she wanted them to find in her services a reflection of the compassionate love of God.

In identifying as far as possible with the poor, Elizabeth faced misunderstanding and contempt from her social peers.

[1] p. 37 L. Lavelle: *The Meaning of Holiness* Burnes & Oates 1951

John of the Cross points out that the apostolic life is a life of contempt, and that of necessity. It is a life that is bound to be misunderstood by the 'wise' of this world.

To be an apostle, to be completely at God's disposal, whether it be for prayer or work, serving wherever the need is, means being willing to suffer so that others may have the first place, that their needs be met, that their gifts be nurtured even at the expense of one's own. But this made Elizabeth ravishingly happy. Conrad states that many saw her at prayer totally transformed, her face radiant. She was a fulfilled woman who knew how to pour herself out in love and self giving.

Because Elizabeth shared in St. Francis' charism there are in both saints all the marks of a simplicity that cannot be divided by reason or effort. It is a combination of purity and ardour, illumined by grace.

In the end Elizabeth's soul, like that of her mentor, had been unified. Yes, she had had to struggle, and even in the last years of her life she still prayed for three things: for contempt of all earthly goods, for the gift of bearing humiliations cheerfully, and to be free from excessive love for her children. She could tell her maids that she was heard in all this, but the requests show that what she asked for did not come naturally, however successfully she hid her pain.

It was the things that could have hindered her progress that Elizabeth transmuted at a glance. Her gaze was upon God – 'My God and my All' – and so she ran singing towards her goal. With Francis she could say, 'The good to which I aspire is so great that all my suffering is turned to joy'.

Nevertheless, this state of renunciation is not attained in a flash. It depends on the day by day acceptance of life, without asserting one's preferences. It means allowing God to fill each moment with persons who need to be cherished and loved. It means responding graciously to daily demands. Then, little by little, the natural aversions of heart and flesh, as with Francis' previous aversion to lepers, are turned into tenderness and active sympathy even for the most secret infirmities in oneself and others.

In Francis and Elizabeth we see people facing the problem

of evil: not with denial, not with direct combat, but with a confrontation in love which leads everything back to the source where alone there is true nourishment: God.

Likewise the bitterness, the sorrow, the pain that each person experiences in life holds a promise of resurrection. To live the Paschal mystery with Francis and Elizabeth is to look beyond the present moment to the point where, as Julian of Norwich so succinctly says: 'All shall be brought to joy'. Nothing is wasted, nothing disposable. All is accepted, treasured and transmuted into life-giving love: even sin, failure and grief.

A heart for the world

I give you a new commandment, that you love one another.
Just as I have loved you, you should also love one another.
By this everyone will know that you are my disciples,
if you have love for one another.
Jn. 13:34-35

The creatvity of the early Third Order women is amazing. Elizabeth is not a foundress in the ordinary sense. She cannot be said to have instituted an Order of nuns or even an Order of nursing sisters; such a thing was unheard of in her time. But she inaugurated a way of being in which it is her *heart* that inspires others to 'go and do likewise' in whatever situation they find themselves and wherever the need lies.

Women like Margaret of Cortona and Angela of Foligno, looking to St. Francis as their inspiration, also discovered the path of poverty and service in their own place; as midwife, as leper nurse, and as women of prayer and penitence with wide influence. It was precisely because they wished to remain free of the structures that hampered the exercise of charity towards their neighbour that they did not choose a monastic form of life but one closer to that of the friars. Hence they did not have the honour accorded to a nun, rather they were true 'sisters', to one another and to the people. They had the honour that flows from freedom and availability, an honour not accorded to their state of life as such but to the intrinsic core of their being: as women, as Franciscans, and above all as Christians.

This could be encapsulated in the legend of St. Elizabeth whereby she is often depicted with a kirtle full of roses. According to the story Elizabeth was one day taking bread to the poor when her husband rode by and saw her. He reined in his horse and angrily demanded to see what she was concealing in the folds of her gown. Afraid to reveal the bread, Elizabeth demurred. Louis insisted. Playing for time, Elizabeth told him she was only carrying a few flowers. Louis pulled the kirtle open to see for himself and, lo and behold, there were indeed only roses, a great profusion of beautiful blooms; the bread had disappeared.

This popular legend is told also of Elizabeth of Portugal, grand niece of our Elizabeth, and it accords much more with what we know of the character of her jealous and unfaithful husband, King Denis. Louis, as all the chronicles attest, allowed Elizabeth to exercise her charity freely, giving 'a completely ungrudging assent to all she did' (the words are those of Conrad of Marburg). The legend as we have it is a much later accretion to her story and is found in none of the early accounts of her life.

However, if we look at the deeper meaning of the story we can grasp the truth it embodies. Elizabeth walked the streets to give bread, i.e. basic necessities, to those in need. She was concerned in nourishing others as Jesus had nourished them; with bread for the body as much as bread for the soul. It was all outwardly so ordinary and so easily misunderstood. What could a woman of Elizabeth's social standing want with the poor? Maybe she was impoverishing her own family to feed outsiders! And what was a woman doing acting with such independence when she should be safely at home under her husband's authority? She must be called to account by the man to whom she should have been subservient and from whom she should have asked permission before venturing forth.

But God vindicated Elizabeth's love-errand. In his eyes what she bore was something beautiful rather than something basic and prosaic. The roses that spilled from her lap were the symbols of a love that could not be confined within the limits of what would be considered reasonable. It was the extravagant gesture of love repaid by the divine Lover himself.

This extravagance motivates the Franciscan sister who, even today, goes under Elizabeth's patronage to the marginalised, the dispossessed, the starving. It is a love that brooks no limits, is beyond the reasonable and the 'safe'. It is present too in those married women whose devotion to husband and children is not a confining but an extending experience. And Elizabeth is an inspiration to those whose place in the Church lies in actual poverty, handicap, sickness. They too are precious and beloved, called to give of themselves in their own limited sphere. They reflect Christ in a special way because to receive love is as, if not more, important than being able to give it.

And what of Elizabeth's heart, the secret of her life? That is a mystery hidden with Christ in God. We can look upon her and see one aspect of the face of Christ. That is enough and more than enough for sainthood, and that is open to us all, if we really want it.

> Let every creature in heaven and on earth,
> in the sea and in the depths,
> give praise, glory, honour and blessing to
> Him who suffered so much for us,
> Who has given so many good things,
> and Who will continue to do so for the future,
> For He is our power and our strength,
> He Who alone is good, Who is most high,
> Who is all powerful, admirable and glorious;
> Who alone is holy, praiseworthy and blessed
> throughout endless ages. Amen.

St. Francis of Assisi.

Appendix

The present rule of the Franciscan Third Order Regular

Chapter one

In the name of the Lord! Here begins the Rule and Life of the Brothers and Sisters of the Third Order Regular of St. Francis.

1. This is the form of life of the Brothers and Sisters of the Third Order Regular of St. Francis: to observe the holy gospel of our Lord Jesus Christ, by living in obedience, in poverty and in chastity. As followers of Jesus Christ after the example of St. Francis, they are obliged to make more and greater efforts to observe the precepts and counsels of our Lord Jesus Christ. They are bound to deny themselves as each has promised to God.

2. The Brothers and Sisters of this Order, like everyone who desires to serve the Lord in the holy, catholic and apostolic Church, resolve to persevere in true faith and penance, because there is no other way to be saved. They desire to live this evangelical conversion in a spirit of prayer, poverty and humility. For this reason they must keep away from all evil and go on doing good to the end. For the Son of God will come again in glory, and he will say to all who have acknowledged and worshipped him, and served him in penance: Come, you whom my Father has blessed, take for your heritage the kingdom prepared for you since the foundation of the world.

3. The Brothers and Sisters promise obedience to the Pope and to the Catholic Church. In the same spirit they are to obey those who have been entrusted with the service of authority in the fraternity. Wherever they are and in whatever place they meet, the Brothers and Sisters should greet and honour one another fervently and from the heart. They should foster unity and fellowship with all members of the Franciscan Family.

Chapter two

Reception into this way of life

4. Those who under the Lord's inspiration, wishing to take up this way of life, are to he received with kindness. At the appropriate time they are to be presented to the ministers who have the authority to admit them.

5. The ministers must make sure that the aspirants truly adhere to the Catholic faith and the sacraments of the Church. If they have the qualities, they are to be introduced to the life of the fraternity. Then everything about this gospel way of life is to be carefully explained to them, especially these words of the Lord: If you wish to be perfect, go sell all that you own and give the money to the poor, and you will have treasure in heaven; then come, follow me; and: If anyone wants to be a follower of mine, let him renounce himself and take up his cross and follow me.

6. So, under the Lord's guidance, let them set out on a life of penance, knowing that we are all obliged to constant conversion of heart. As a sign of their conversion and consecration to the gospel life, they are to wear poor clothes and lead a simple life.

7. At the end of the period of formation they are to be received into obedience, promising to observe this rule and life always. They should cast away all cares and anxiety and be concerned how best to serve, love, reverence and adore the Lord God, with an honest heart and a devout mind.

8. Let them always make a home and dwelling place in themselves for him who is the Lord God Almighty, Father, Son and Holy Spirit. Thus, with undivided hearts, they may grow in all-embracing love, as they turn without ceasing towards God and their neighbour.

Chapter three

The Spirit of Prayer

9. All over the world, in every place, at every hour and every moment, the Brothers and Sisters should believe truly and humbly. In their hearts they should cherish, love, reverence, adore, serve, praise, bless and glorify the most high and supreme, eternal God, Father, Son and Holy Spirit. They should adore him with all their heart because we ought always to pray and not lose heart. The Father seeks such worshippers. In this spirit, in union with the whole Church, the Brothers and Sisters should celebrate the Liturgy of the Hours.

The Brothers and Sisters whom the Lord has called to a life of contemplation should show forth their dedication to God with renewed joy each day and celebrate the love which the Father has for the whole world, who created us, redeemed us and who out of his mercy alone will save us.

10. The Brothers and Sisters should praise the Lord, the King of heaven and earth, in union with all his creatures. They should give him thanks because by his own holy will and through his only Son, with the Holy Spirit, he created all things spiritual and material, and he made us in his own image and likeness.

11. The Brothers and Sisters are to conform themselves totally to the holy gospel. Therefore they should keep in mind and meditate on the words of our Lord Jesus Christ, who is the Word of the Father, and on the words of the Holy Spirit, which are spirit and life.

12. They should take part in the sacrifice of our Lord Jesus Christ and receive his Body and Blood with great humility and reverence, recalling the words of the Lord: Anyone who eats my flesh and drinks my blood has eternal life.

They must show all reverence and honour, as much as they are able for the most holy Body and Blood of our Lord Jesus Christ and for his most holy name and written words. In him all things in heaven and on earth have been brought to peace and reconciled with Almighty God.

13. For all their sins the Brothers and Sisters should do penance without delay, inwardly by sorrow and outwardly by confession, and they should bring forth worthy fruits of penance. They should fast, and strive to be always simple and humble. They should desire nothing else except our Saviour who offered himself by his own blood on the altar of the cross, as a sacrifice and victim for our sins. He left us an example so that we might follow in his footsteps.

Chapter four

The life of chastity for the sake of the kingdom of heaven

14. The Brothers and Sisters should keep in mind the great dignity with which the Lord has endowed them, 'for he created and formed' them 'in the image of his beloved Son as to the body, and in his own likeness as to the spirit'. Created through Christ in him, they have chosen this form of life which is based on the teaching and life of our Redeemer.

15. Professing chastity for the sake of the kingdom of heaven, they should be solicitous for the things of the Lord and they 'have nothing else to do except to follow the will of the Lord and to please him'. They should conduct themselves in everything, so that love for God and everyone in the world may shine forth in all that they do.

16. They should remember that they have been called by the sublime gift of grace to show forth in their lives the wonderful mystery of the Church, whereby the Church is joined with Christ, her divine Spouse.

17. Above all, they should keep before them the example of the most blessed Virgin Mary, Mother of God and our Lord Jesus Christ. They are to do this in accordance with the command of St. Francis who had a deep devotion for Holy Mary, Lady and Queen, the Virgin who became the Church. And they should remember that they are to follow the example of the Virgin Mary who called herself the handmaid of the Lord.

Chapter five

The way to serve and work

18. The Brothers and Sisters to whom the Lord has given the grace of serving others or working, should serve and work faithfully and devotedly, like the poor. Let them beware of idleness which is the enemy of the soul. In their service and work they should not extinguish the spirit of holy prayer and devotion, which all earthly things are meant to foster.

19. In return for their work they may accept what is necessary for their material needs and those of their Brothers and Sisters. They should accept it humbly as is rightfully expected of God's servants and followers of most high poverty. What they have over they should give to the poor. They should never want to be in charge of others. On the contrary, they should be servants and, for the Lord's sake, be subject to every human creature.

20. The Brothers and Sisters should be meek, peaceful and unassuming, gentle and humble, speaking courteously to everyone, as is right. Wherever they are and wherever they go in the world they are not to quarrel, get into arguments or condemn others. Rather they should show that they are joyful in the Lord, good-humoured and gracious, as is right. When they greet others, they should say: 'The Lord give you peace'.

Chapter six

The life of poverty

21. All the Brothers and Sisters must strive to follow the humility and poverty of our Lord Jesus Christ. Though he was rich beyond measure, he chose poverty in this world as did his mother, the Blessed Virgin Mary; and he emptied himself. Let them remember that we are to have nothing of this world except food and clothing; let us be content with that, as St. Paul says. They should be profoundly suspicious of money. Let them rejoice when they live among the outcast and despised, among the poor and the

weak, the sick and the lepers, and those who beg in the streets.

22. The truly poor in spirit, following the example of the Lord, neither possess nor defend anything as their own. They live in this world as pilgrims and strangers. This is the summit of the most exalted poverty which makes us heirs and kings of the kingdom of heaven. It has made us poor in earthly goods, but has raised us high in virtue. Let this be our heritage which leads into the land of the living. Holding fast to this, for the name of our Lord Jesus Christ, may we never want to have anything else under heaven.

Chapter seven

Fraternal Life

23. Because of God's love, the Brothers and Sisters should love one another, as the Lord says: This is my commandment, that you love one another as I have loved you. Let them show by their actions that they love one another. With confidence let them make their needs known to one another, so that each may find what is needed and all may serve one another. They are blessed who love their brethren as much when these are sick and cannot repay them, as when they are well and can repay them. No matter what happens to them, they should give thanks to the Creator. They should desire for themselves whatever the Lord wills for them, be it to be healthy or sick.

24. If disharmony arises among them because of something said or done, they should ask forgiveness of one another at once with humility, before they offer their gift of prayer to the Lord. If any Brothers or Sisters gravely transgress the form of life they have professed, the minister or others who may know about it, should admonish them. In doing so they should cause them no shame, nor speak evil about them, but show them great kindness. They must all be very careful not to be angry or vexed on account of anyone's sin, because anger and vexation hinder love in themselves and in others.

Chapter eight

The obedience of love

25. According to the example of the Lord Jesus, who sacrificed his own will to the will of the Father, the Brothers and Sisters should remember that they have renounced their own wills for God's sake. In all the chapters they hold let them seek first the kingdom of God and his justice, and exhort one another to observe with greater dedication the rule they have professed and to follow faithfully in the footsteps of our Lord Jesus Christ. No one is to have power or dominate over others. Through love all should serve and obey one another willingly. This is the true and holy obedience of our Lord Jesus Christ.

26. They are always bound to have one of their members as minister and servant of the fraternity, whom they are strictly obliged to obey in everything they have promised the Lord to observe, and which is not against their conscience and this rule.

27. Those who are ministers and servants of the others, should visit them, and with humility and love advise and encourage them. Wherever there are Brothers and Sisters who know and acknowledge that they cannot observe the rule spiritually, they can and ought to have recourse to their ministers. The ministers, for their part, should receive them with love and kindness and show them such friendship, that these Brothers and Sisters can speak and treat with them as would masters with their servants. For so it should be, that the ministers be the servants of everyone.

28. No one is to appropriate any ministry. On the contrary, those who hold an office should relinquish it gladly at the appointed time.

Chapter nine

The Apostolic Life

29. The Brothers and Sisters shall love the Lord with all their heart, and with all their soul and mind and with all their strength, and they shall love their neighbour as themselves. Let them glorify the Lord in all that they do. He has sent them into the world to bear witness by word and deed to his voice and to proclaim to everyone that he alone is the Almighty Lord.

30. As they proclaim peace with their lips, they must have it to overflowing in their hearts. No one should be provoked to anger or offended because of them. On the contrary, everyone should be drawn to peace, kindness and friendship by their gentleness. The Brothers and Sisters have been called to heal the wounded, mend the broken and bring back those who have gone astray. Wherever they are let them remember that they have given themselves to the Lord Jesus Christ and pledged their whole life to him. For love of him they must face every enemy, seen and unseen, because the Lord says: Blessed are those who suffer persecution in the cause of right, theirs is the kingdom of heaven.

31. In the love which is God, let all the Brothers and Sisters whether at prayer, or serving others, or working, strive to have humility in all things. They are not to boast, not to be self-satisfied, and not to pride themselves in their heart for the good they do by word or deed, not even for the good which God sometimes does or speaks and accomplishes in and through them. No matter where they are, in all circumstances, they must acknowledge that every good belongs to the Lord God Almighty the Ruler of all things; and they must thank him from whom all good things come.

Exhortation and Blessing

32. Let all the Brothers and Sisters bear in mind that above everything else they should desire to have the spirit of the Lord and his holy grace.

Always obedient to the holy Church, and steadfast in the Catholic faith, let them observe, as they have firmly promised, the poverty, and the humility, and the gospel of our Lord Jesus Christ.

May all who observe these things be filled in heaven with the blessing of the most high Father, and on earth with the blessing of his beloved Son, with, the most Holy Spirit, the Comforter, and with all the powers of heaven, and with all that is holy. And I, Brother Francis, your poor, little servant, as much as I am able, confirm for you, within and without, this most holy blessing.

Translation by Father Eric Doyle OFM.
Used with kind permission of the Order of Friars Minor.

Bibliography

Ancelet-Hustache, Jeame: *Gold Tried by Fire. Saint Elizabeth of Hungary.* Chicago Herald Press 1963.
Arnold, Bro. : *The Book of the Visions and Instructions of Bl. Angela of Foligno.* Translated by a Secular Priest. Richardson 1871.
Chesterton, G. K. : *St. Francis of Assisi.* Hodder and Stoughton 1923.
Congar, Yves: 'St, Elizabeth and the Charity of the Cross' in *Vie Spirituelle,* Jan. 1932.
Coudenhove, Ida: *The Nature of Sanctity.* Trans. Ruth Bonsell and E. I. Watkin. Sheed and Ward 1932.
Engelbert, Omer: *St. Francis of Assisi.* Burns and Oates 1950.
Focillon, Henri: *The Art of the West II: Gothic.* Phaidon Press 1963.
Francis and Clare: *Complete Works.* R. Armstrong & I Brady. Paulist Press 1982.
Habig, Itrion O. F. M. : *The History of the Third Order of St. Francis.* Franciscan Herald Press, N. Y, 1947.
John of the Cross: *Complete Works.* Trans. David Lewis. Longman Green 1864.
Lavelle, Louis: *The Meaning of Holiness.* Burns and Oates 1951.
Nigg, W. : *Francis of Assisi.* Mowbrays 1975.
Raymond, E. : *In the Steps of St. Francis.* Rich and Cowan Ltd. 1938.
Seesholtz, A. : *St. Elizabeth. Her Brother's Keeper.* New York Philosophical Library, 1948.
Southern, R. W. : *Westen Society and the Church in the Middle Ages.* Penguin, 1970.
Stein, Edith: 'The Spirit of St. Elizabeth', in *Collected Works Vol. IV.* Trans. W. Stein. I. C. S. Publns. 1987.
Wenrich, F. J. von: *St. Elizabeth of Hungary.* Trans, I. J. Collins Burns, Oates and Washbourne 1933.
Voillaum, R. : *Christian Vocation.* Darton, Longman and Todd 1973.